houses and gardens of
kyoto

Photography by Akihiko Seki

Text by Thomas Daniell

With a new foreword by Matthew Stavros

TUTTLE PUBLISHING

Tokyo • Rutland, Vermont • Singapore

CONTENTS

Kyoto's Unique Architectural Heritage

Opposite A room inside the Kachoden reception hall at Shoren-in (page 70).

Kyoto is a place that evokes tremendous fascination and admiration. It is a city of great natural beauty and virtually countless architectural treasures. In Japanese poetry and prose, no other single location has been celebrated as frequently or as floridly as Kyoto. It has one of the highest concentrations of Buddhist temples in the world and boasts as many as seventeen UNESCO World Heritage sites. Because it was the only major Japanese city not subjected to widespread bombardment during the Second World War, many of the wooden buildings, narrow byways, and shops have survived to give it a distinctly traditional flavor.

Visitors cannot be blamed for flocking to Kyoto's many grand temples and shrines. Their monumental halls and towering pagodas inspire awe and command respect. But one should not let the imposing gables, giant Buddhas and cast bronze bells blind them to a quieter and less pretentious, yet ultimately more distinctive side to this great historical city. To really experience Kyoto—not just see or admire it—one must venture into the living quarters, sit still by a stone or moss garden, and sip tea while bathed in the soft light that filters through hand-made paper screens. There, one comes face to face with the stories and personalities that assembled the city and built its unique culture.

But these remarkable places are not always easy to find or accessible, and the people of Kyoto are famous for having jealously guarded them throughout history. Through the publication of this book, however, Akihiko Seki and Thomas Daniell have drawn back the curtains (or shall I say "paper screens?") and provided a refreshingly comprehensive glimpse into the heart of the city. *Houses and Gardens of Kyoto* achieves something special by presenting a visual and descriptive vantage that is not merely appealing and smart, it is true to Kyoto's culture. The images capture the striking juxtaposition of a built landscape that is at once new and old, meticulously refined and methodically neglected. The text returns again and again to this critical theme, providing insights into Japanese aesthetics found in no other single volume.

The perspective is honest and unmistakably human. Whether it be the gardens of Ginkaku-ji or the famous tea room at the Katsura Imperial Villa, readers might imagine themselves enjoying the view from the slightly elevated seating position afforded by *seiza*, the traditional Japanese sitting style. Attention to detail is also striking and quintessentially Kyotoesque. Note, for example, the several photographs of slippers placed carefully outside doorways. Although unremarkable in their own right, visitors to Kyoto will know that a host's attention to such seemingly small matters exemplifies the spirit of Japanese hospitality expressed by the word *motenashi*.

From the viewpoint of someone who has spent over twenty years researching Kyoto's urban history, what makes this book so unique and valuable is its apparent refusal, conscious or not, to separate houses and gardens into distinct categories or sections. To do so would be to commit a quiet violence against the city's architectural tradition. To be sure, in Kyoto, the two comprise a single, seamless whole that cannot and should not be dissolved. Seki and Daniell were clearly aware of this fundamental trait when they planned a book that is remarkable in both content and form. Its beautiful photographs and penetrating text transport the reader and provide a vantage onto Kyoto's unique urban history that is accessible, intelligent and enchanting.

Houses and Gardens of Kyoto

Left The central gate along the main garden path in the Okouchi Sanso estate.

Right The Kinkaku, or Golden Pavilion, is now part of Rokuon-ji temple, but was originally the Buddhist relic hall in the retirement villa of Shogun Ashikaga Yoshimitsu.

Page 1 The *genkan* (entrance hall) at Kinmata (page 108).

Page 2 The entrance to the Tekisuian tea house at Okouchi Sanso (page 178).

Page 4 A detail of the *byobu* (folding screen) affixed to a wall at Iori Zaimoku-cho (page 128).

Kyoto (or Heian-kyo, as the city was named at its founding by Emperor Kammu in 794) has been the birthplace—the incubator and crucible—of most what is now considered to be quintessential Japanese culture. Afflicted by fires, wars, typhoons, floods, and earthquakes, Kyoto was razed and rebuilt more than once during its thousand years as the capital of Japan, yet it has also witnessed extraordinary flowerings of stylistic invention in literature and theater, ceramics and calligraphy, clothing and cuisine, and, not least, architecture and gardens. Much of this coalesced in the fifteenth century as what is now collectively known as *higashiyama bunka* (east mountain culture), during which the arts became suffused by the Zen-inspired aesthetic of *wabi sabi* (best translated as "impoverished beauty"): the *chado* tea ceremony, ikebana flower arrangement, *sumi-e* ink painting, *no* theater, and so on. "Flowering" is indeed the right word; the definitive Kyoto aesthetic and attitude is known as *hannari*, literally "to become a flower." The goal—for people as well as artifacts—is to be elegant yet understated, vibrant yet delicate, and always exquisitely sensitive to the nuances of one's surroundings. For all the damage that has occurred over the centuries, for all the relentless modernization still taking place today, Kyoto remains a rich, inexhaustible archive of Japanese cultural history.

On the site of what was in prehistoric times an enormous lake,

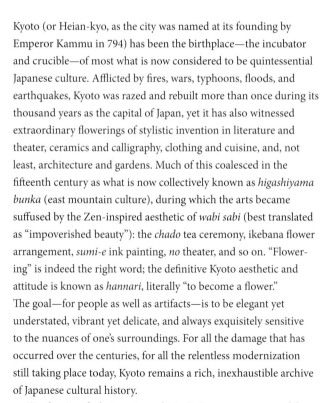

Kyoto occupies a flat plain surrounded by a horseshoe of mountains open to the south—a secluded locale and climate judged to have ideal geomantic properties. Emperor Kammu paid token compensation to the local farmers that he forced to relocate, and then had the city laid out on a regular gridiron pattern comprising walled blocks called *cho*, each a 120 by 120 square meters (40 by 40 *jo* in the traditional measurement system). Influenced by city planning models from China, Kyoto was intended as an ideal city *ex nihilo*, a kind of urban mandala or matrix that placed the Emperor as an intermediary between the gods and the citizens. Inevitably, the purity of the original vision was compromised by topography and distorted by demographics. Over the ensuing centuries, the city has ebbed and flowed across the land, shifting eastward and regenerating in the aftermath of intermittent destruction. The present layout of Kyoto largely dates from the late-sixteenth century, when the city was reconfigured and rebuilt by Toyotomi Hideyoshi (1536–98), an extraordinary figure who rose from peasant origins to become the unifier and ruler of Japan after centuries of unrest and civil war.

Kyoto's residential architecture evolved gradually from the founding of the city onward, and has been retrospectively classified into three main stylistic subdivisions: *shinden zukuri* (palace style), *shoin zukuri* (study style), and *sukiya zukuri* (tea house style).

Rather than distinct historical stages, these form a continuous evolution of shared themes, following a general progression from a somewhat rigid and monumental formality to a more emancipated and sophisticated eclecticism. Not quite styles in the strict art-historical sense, they reflect particular lifestyles and social stratifications. Though primarily intended for the nobility and aristocracy, these three architectural types have also influenced the design of *minka*, the traditional vernacular houses of the general population. The *minka* may be broadly subdivided into urban dwellings (machiya townhouses, *nagaya* rowhouses, and *yashiki* detached manors) and rural dwellings (noka farmhouses, *gyoka* fisherfolk dwellings, and *sanka* mountain huts), all of which comprise wooden post-and-beam structures surfaced with a variety of natural materials.

During the early Heian Period (794–1185), members of the aristocracy moved from all across the country to the new capital, where they built houses in the *shinden* style. Though commoners inhabited small subdivisions of a city block, a *shinden* dwelling often occupied an entire block, and in some cases two or even four blocks. Within perimeter fences made of tamped earth and capped with tiles, the north half of the site would contain a roughly symmetrical array of pavilions linked by large sheltered corridors, arranged to contain a central courtyard that faced onto a garden and pond located to the south. The main building was the *shinden* itself, used for the daily life of the master of the house, with *tainoya* (secondary pavilions) for other family members and servants. The

buildings lacked ceilings or internal partitions, their interior spaces articulated only by freestanding folding panels called *byobu*. The outer perimeters were closed by means of *shitomido* (detachable wooden panels), making the interiors completely dark at night and completely open to the environment during the day. Aside from a few movable tatami mats used for sleeping or sitting, the floors were wooden boards. No original *shinden* residences survive today, but their general characteristics are known from ancient picture scrolls and archaeological excavations. Some structures within the Kyoto Imperial Palace precinct (a reconstruction built in the nineteenth century) give a good sense of the *shinden* style, as does the Heian Jingu shrine (a partial, reduced-scale replica of the original Heian-kyo Imperial Palace).

As effective political power shifted from the Imperial family to the samurai warriors during the Muromachi Period (1336–1573), samurai families adopted the courtly lifestyle manifested in the *shinden* style while adapting the dwellings to suit their own needs. Samurai were expected to become monks upon their retirement, so a number of distinctive elements intended to facilitate a life of scholarship appeared, such as the *tokonoma* (decorative alcove), *chigaidana* (staggered shelves), and *tsukeshoin* (built-in writing desk). These were initially contained in an annex that appeared as a component of the transitional *shuden* style, through which the *shinden* style evolved into the relatively opulent and formal *shoin* style of houses for both aristocrats and abbots. Made up of pavilions comprising an *omoya* (central volume) surrounded by

houses and gardens of kyoto

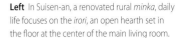
hisashi (peripheral corridors), a *shoin*-style residence had a relatively free and asymmetric arrangement within its site. The floors became entirely covered with tatami mats, and wooden ceiling panels hid the roof beams. The cylindrical wooden pillars found in the *shinden* style were replaced with square pillars known as *kakubashira*, making it easier to divide rooms by installing a range of newly invented sliding fittings: shoji (translucent paper), *fusuma* (opaque paper), *sugido* (wooden panels made of Japanese cedar), and *mairado* (wooden panels with rows of horizontal wooden crosspieces). The *shikidai* vestibule, with a wooden floor set at a slightly lower level than the tatami rooms, arose as the predecessor to the modern *genkan* entrance hall. The *shoin* style continued to develop over time, attaining its definitive form during the Edo Period (1603–1868) as exemplified by Kyoto's Nijo Castle, residence of the Tokugawa shoguns.

The next key development was the *soan chashitsu* (rustic tea house), a small hut for holding tea ceremonies, created during the Azuchi Momoyama Period (1573–1603). The custom of *chanoyu* (drinking tea) had been introduced to Japan from China many centuries earlier, and was refined in the Zen temples of Kyoto into a precise ritual: *chado*, the "way of tea." The practice became fashionable among the aristocracy, who competed in the accumulation of expensive tea ceremony utensils from China and Korea, and gradually gained in popularity with the general public. The tea ceremony tended to be an elaborate performance before a large audience, held in a partitioned-off section of a *shoin*-style room decorated with an opulence that bordered on vulgarity. It was the Zen Buddhist priest Murata Shuko (1422–1502) who introduced the radical innovation of an intimate gathering in which the host himself served the tea, thus creating the basis for the tea ceremony as it is known today.

The sixteenth century saw the appearance of a room solely used for tea ceremonies, generally with an area of *yojohan* (four and a half tatami mats, about 7.3 square meters), just enough to hold the

host and a few guests. This became the prototype for the *soan chashitsu*, the design of which was perfected by the celebrated tea master Sen no Rikyu (1522–91), *chado* advisor to Hideyoshi himself. Implicitly rejecting the flamboyance of tea ceremony practices among the aristocracy, the *soan chashitsu* is intended for a version of the tea ceremony known as *wabicha*, which emphasizes simplicity, humility, and frugality. Seemingly temporary huts with thatch roofs, wall surfaces of exposed dirt, and wooden elements left in their natural state, these tea houses deliberately recall the impoverished dwellings of ancient Buddhist hermits. While still using many of the elements found in *shoin* design—tatami mats, *tokonoma* alcoves, shoji screens—the designs emphasized idiosyncrasy and irregularity, assiduously avoiding repetition and standardization. The ostentatious Chinese implements were substituted with inexpensive, imperfect, everyday Japanese items, albeit selected with exquisite taste. Though an extension of Zen Buddhist practices, the *soan chashitsu* was empty of religious icons, creating a condensed aesthetic experience of natural materials, their austerity and asperity enhanced by the subtle play of light and shadow.

In a sense, the tea ceremony is considered a form of Zen practice, as expressed in the phrase *chazen ichimi*: "tea and Zen have the same flavor." Introverted and hermetic, the *soan chashitsu* is nonetheless inseparable from the garden in which it is located. The

roji (dewy ground) path leading through the garden is intended as a transition from the prosaic world of everyday life to the poetic world of the tea ceremony. Tea gardens tend to be verdant, with overhanging leaves and mossy ground, though without the distraction of brightly colored flowers. Guests follow an artistically composed array of stepping stones—Rikyu stated that they should be 60 percent functional and 40 percent ornamental—passing a *toro* (stone lantern) and *tsukubai* (stone water basin) to arrive at the *koshikake machiai* waiting area. Having been welcomed by the host, they pass through the tiny *nijiriguchi* entrance. The space inside also tended to be tiny—the single surviving example of a *soan chashitsu* believed to have been designed by Rikyu is only two tatami mats (3.2 square meters) in area. Called Tai-an, it was built in 1582 on the grounds of his residence in Kyoto, but later disassembled and rebuilt at Myoki-an temple, just south of the city.

The understated eclecticism of the *soan chashitsu* influenced the next major shift in Kyoto's residential architecture, the *sukiya* style (which is more properly called *sukiya fu shoin zukuri*: the *shoin* style as influenced by the *sukiya*). Used interchangeably with *chashitsu* as a name for the tea house itself, *sukiya* is an emancipated and idiosyncratic variation on the *shoin* style. The atmosphere is more relaxed, the spaces smaller, the ceilings lower, the elements thinner, the materials untreated, the compositions

houses and gardens of kyoto

Left The Botan-no-ma (Peony Room) of Daikaku-ji temple, in which eighteen *fusuma* panels have been covered with paintings of peonies.

Right The *karesansui* (dry landscape) garden adjacent to the large hall in Nanzen-ji incorporates the distant Higashiyama mountains as *shakkei* (borrowed scenery).

relatively uninhibited. To be sure, *sukiya* architecture often includes whimsical decorative elements at odds with the austere *wabicha* aesthetic, and rather than the isolated microcosm of the tea house, typical *sukiya* architecture tends to be open to, and integrated with, its environment; indeed, the surrounding garden should be regarded as a necessary complement to the building. The *sukiya* style reached its apotheosis with the Katsura Rikyu Imperial Villa, built in the seventeenth century, but has dominated residential design right up until the modern period and continues to be popular today. While the vast majority of *sukiya* dwellings still retain some purely *shoin*-style spaces—the *shoin* rooms are for important occasions and guests, whereas the *sukiya* rooms are for daily life and friends—it is with the *sukiya* style that traditional Japanese architecture attained its fullest maturity and refinement. The underlying modular system of dimensionally coordinated timber frames and infill panels provides a disciplined framework for creations of extraordinary delicacy. Lightweight walls and sliding panels produce fluid, mutable interiors, while the peripheral *engawa* (veranda) spaces and their layers of lattices and screens enable a flexible integration of outside and inside. Suffused with soft light through mobile shoji panels and open *ranma* slots above the interior partitions, the predominantly rectilinear patterns that define each surface are accentuated by occasional irregular

elements, such as the naturally twisted form of the *tokobashira* corner post in the *tokonoma* alcove.

While the suffix *ya* simply means "house," the prefix *suki* has been written using various kanji characters across the centuries, phonetically identical but different in meaning. Initially *suki* used the kanji character 好, meaning "fondness," and acclaimed aesthetes would be described as *sukisha*: people with a fine sense of assurance and discrimination in their aesthetic choices. Generally wealthy members of the aristocracy or nobility with time on their hands, *sukisha* were devoted to the full range of the arts, which were considered to reach a unified apotheosis in the tea ceremony and its associated implements and spaces. Thus a *sukiya* was a building designed not only according to personal taste, but according to the exceptional taste of a *sukisha*. During the Muromachi Period (1336–1573), *suki* came to be written using the two kanji characters 数奇, which are simply a reversal of the kanji for *kisu* (奇数 "odd number"), thus evoking irregularity or eccentricity. Indeed, in contrast with the Chinese love of even numbers, and hence symmetry and balance, Japanese culture is pervaded by a preference for the asymmetry and tension implied by odd numbers. Gift giving in Japan entails odd-numbered amounts of money bound by cords with an odd number of strands, given on odd-numbered anniversaries. The *shichi-go-san* (seven-

five-three) shrine visits are made by children of those ages to celebrate passage into each successive phase of childhood. The doubling of an odd number is even more auspicious: the *gosekku* (five seasonal festivals) are held on the first day of the first month, the third day of the third month, the fifth day of the fifth month, and so on. This predilection for odd numbers underlies all traditional Japanese aesthetics. A *haiku* poem, for example, comprises seventeen syllables divided 5/7/5, and *waka* classic verse comprises thirty-one syllables divided 5/7/5-7/7. The renowned Ryoan-ji stone garden contains three rock clusters, comprising three, five, and seven rocks respectively, and all fifteen can never be seen simultaneously—from any given viewpoint, at least one is hidden behind the others. Simultaneously insufficient and excessive, an odd number cannot be balanced or resolved without leaving a remainder—an intimation of the existence of something more than the immediately perceptible. It is this disquieting sense of incompletion that gives tension and dissonance to all the traditional arts, whether the laconic simplicity of *haiku*, the spontaneous black brush strokes on white paper in a *sumi-e* painting, the incongruous twisted branches in ikebana, or the irregular accents and subtle misalignments in *sukiya* architecture. Such serene yet precariously suspended compositions always rely on the intuition and imagination of the observer for their completion.

Selected by Japanese photographer Akihiko (Alan) Seki, this book contains a collection of houses in the widest sense of the word: exemplars, variations, and hybrids of the *shinden*, *shoin*, and *sukiya* styles, with buildings ranging from summer villas for the aristocracy to townhouses for ordinary citizens, from monumental Buddhist temples to insubstantial garden huts, and from personal homes to traditional inns. All have their related gardens, whether *tsuboniwa* (condensed courtyard gardens), *kaiyushiki teien* (picturesque stroll gardens), *karesansui* ("dry landscape") stone gardens, *shakkei* (the "borrowed scenery" of a distant landscape), or some combination of these and other types. Each one is a fine example of traditional Kyoto house and garden design, yet to discuss the historical origins of this architecture is not as straightforward as it may seem. Take, for example, the gold leaf-clad Kinkaku (known in English as the Golden Pavilion), one of Kyoto's most famous and spectacular structures. Built in 1397 as part of a retirement villa for Shogun Ashikaga Yoshimitsu and later incorporated into the Zen Buddhist temple Rokuon-ji (otherwise known as Kinkaku-ji), it is thanks to buildings such as this one that Kyoto was mostly spared from damage during the Second World War. Though considered as a possible target for the atomic bomb that ultimately landed on Hiroshima, Kyoto was recognized as a city of such profound cultural importance that US Secretary of War Henry L. Stimson declared it to be "the one city that they must not

bomb without my permission." Yet throughout the war one of the young acolytes living at Rokuon-ji was longing for the bombs to land. He harbored a strange obsession with the Golden Pavilion that could only be consummated by seeing it burn down with him inside. When the war ended with the building still intact, the acolyte made its destruction his mission in life, plotting an act of simultaneous arson and suicide. He was half successful: in 1950, he burned the building to the ground, but lost his nerve and escaped the fire. Quickly arrested, tried, and jailed, he was found to be suffering from various mental and physical illnesses, and died within a few years. The Golden Pavilion, on the other hand, rose from the ashes: a gleaming replica was completed in 1955. There are conflicting opinions regarding the acolyte's true motives (famously fictionalized in Mishima Yukio's novel *The Temple of the Golden Pavilion*), but in any case the building you will see in Kyoto today is not the original Golden Pavilion. In fact, this was not even the first time it had been completely destroyed by fire, and like every wooden building in Japan it has been subject to frequent repair and constant replacement of parts over its lifetime. Very little of the structure has ever been "original" in any conventional sense. Yet in the minds of the Japanese public, the current structure is indeed the real thing; it just happens to be made of new materials.

This demonstrates something quite fundamental about the Japanese attitude toward historical authenticity. Naturally, if the Parthenon were to be destroyed and rebuilt, it would be seen as a substitute for the lost original. In the West, ideas may change but substance should be eternal; in the East, it seems that the opposite is true. Indeed, much of the traditional architecture you will encounter in Kyoto today may be old in form but relatively new in substance. Made of fragile materials—wood, paper, bamboo, earth—subject to a humid climate and frequent natural disasters, these buildings require constant repair. The fabric of the city has its own languid metabolism, a pulse of ongoing construction and destruction, replication and renewal. Manifesting the paradoxical Japanese love of both the patinated and the pristine, these artifacts from the ancient past are suffused with the smell of freshly cut *hinoki* wood and newly laid tatami mats, surrounded by fastidiously manicured hedges and raked gravel. The houses and gardens of Kyoto remain ageless.

Perhaps the most common phrase to be found on a *kakejiku* (hanging scroll) in a *tokonoma* is *ichi go ichi e* ("one occasion, one encounter"). The implication is that every moment is irreducibly unique. Above and beyond historical narratives and cultural intentions, the ineffable spaces, shadows, scents, and sounds of these houses and gardens are best experienced in all their sensual immediacy and intensity, right here and right now.

aristocratic villas

One of the more curious aspects of Imperial rule during Kyoto's thousand-year tenure as capital of Japan is the *insei* (cloistered rule) system, in which an Emperor would officially retire but continue to exert power from behind the scenes. Abdicating at an early age and forcing one of his own children—often no more than an infant—to ascend the Chrysanthemum Throne, the Emperor would take the title of *daijo tenno* (Retired Emperor) or, in cases where he entered the Buddhist priesthood, the title of *daijo hoo* (Cloistered Emperor). It was not unknown for there to be several Retired Emperors living at the same time, but only one would be acknowledged to have authority. For most of Kyoto's history, this was more or less irrelevant anyway: real power lay elsewhere. At the end of the Heian Period (794–1185) it had become generally accepted that the Retired Emperor was ruling with the titular Emperor as a figurehead, yet at that same historical moment effective control of the nation shifted to the military government of the Kamakura Shogunate. From the Kamakura Period (1185–1333) onward, the balance of power continued to oscillate between the military dictators and the Imperial family, but for the most part lay beyond a somewhat farcical series of façades: a nominal Emperor who was controlled by a Retired Emperor who answered to the Shogun who delegated to his military generals.

It was this very lack of ultimate responsibility that allowed the Retired Emperors the freedom to cultivate their hobbies, to study and contribute to the development of arts such as the tea ceremony, flower arrangement, and calligraphy. Imperial wealth was used to sponsor and indulge poets, painters, and sculptors. Those Retired Emperors and other members of the nobility who commissioned retirement villas and summer palaces often collaborated on the designs with the carpenters and gardeners they employed. Produced for the wealthiest clients on the best sites by the most skilful artisans using the highest-grade materials, the aristocratic villas of Kyoto are quintessential examples of the qualities of traditional Japanese architecture.

Katsura Imperial Villa

桂離宮

LOCATION **NISHIGYO-KU**
ESTABLISHED IN **1615**
BUILT FOR **HACHIJONOMIYA TOSHIHITO**

Invariably described as the apotheosis of *sukiya*-style architecture, the buildings and gardens that make up Katsura Imperial Villa in fact display an eclectic hybrid of design approaches. The architecture juxtaposes and intermingles *shoin* and *sukiya* elements and spaces, with even a trace of the *shinden* style in its relationship to the garden and miniature lake. It is, of course, this very heterogeneity that defines Katsura as an exemplar of purest *sukiya*.

One of two surviving Imperial villas located in Kyoto (the other is Shugakuin Imperial Villa), Katsura Imperial Villa was originally built in 1615 as a country residence for Prince Toshihito (1579–1629), a member of the Hachijonomiya family, and later expanded by his son, Prince Toshitada (1619–62). The three main buildings—Koshoin, Chushoin, and Shingoten—were built in stages, cumulatively forming a linked, diagonally stepping composition known as *ganko* (flying geese). As well as reducing the apparent building volume, the subtle dynamism of this arrangement enhances natural light and ventilation inside, and creates intimate relationships with the lake outside. Four unique tea houses are distributed throughout the villa grounds, and the whole comprises a picturesque *kaiyushiki teien* (stroll garden) around the lake. The many historical accounts of visits by members of the nobility to Katsura Imperial Villa invariably mention touring the garden by boat as well as by foot, stopping to admire the view at prescribed locations. Indeed, despite the naturalistic appearance, every part of the garden has been deliberately and precisely composed using a design technique known as *miegakure*, in which various elements alternately disappear and reappear in different aspects as one moves about. Undoubtedly the finest example of the integration of architecture and environment to be found in Japan, Katsura Imperial Villa's complexities and contradictions have allowed observers to interpret it in multiple ways—during the early twentieth century several notable European architects believed they had discovered here a precursor to the modernist simplicity and functionalism they were then pursuing.

Previous spread Interior of Gepparo tea house at Katsura Imperial Villa.

Above The Shoin complex is a series of linked buildings comprising the Koshoin (Old Shoin), Chushoin (Middle Shoin), and Shingoten (New Palace). The small Gakkinoma (Music Room) is interposed between the latter two.

Opposite above The linked Shoin buildings are related to each other in a stepping composition known as *ganko* (flying geese), enhancing natural light and ventilation inside each one.

Opposite below left Made of bamboo, the *tsukimidai* (moon-viewing platform) projects from the large veranda of the Koshoin and gives a superb overview of the garden.

Opposite below right The east entrance to the veranda of the Koshoin, from which the *tsukimidai* extends toward the pond.

Far left above The interior of Shokintei (Pine Lute Pavilion), the first tea house encountered when circumnavigating the Katsura grounds. The tea preparation area is visible on the veranda beyond.

Left above Shokintei is first seen across a stone slab bridge linking two islands in the pond, designed to evoke Amanohashidate, a famous scenic spot on the Japan Sea coast.

Left below The middle room of the oldest tea house at Katsura, Gepparo (Moon Wave Lookout), so named because its elevated location provides a view of the moon's reflection in the pond.

Right The tea preparation area on the veranda of Shokintei, containing a water basin, a hearth for heating water, and a shelf for tea utensils, all screened by a low wall of woven reeds.

Below A glimpse of the famous indigo-and-white checkered pattern in the *tokonoma* of Shokintei.

Above Shokatei (Prize Flower Pavilion) tea house has a raised floor comprising four tatami mats set in a U shape. There is a hearth for boiling water in the foreground and *chigaidana* (staggered shelves) for tea utensils to the rear.

Right Stone paths lead up to Shokatei, which is located at the highest point in the garden.

Right The entrance courtyard of the Koshoin contains an interesting combination of regular and irregular stepping stones. To the left is a stone lantern designed in the style of tea master Furuta Oribe (1543–1615).

Below left The rectangular strip of *ishidatami* stepping stones set adjacent to Sotoshikoshikake (Waiting Bench), where visitors would pause while the host was preparing tea.

Below right A *tsuchibei* fence on the perimeter of the villas grounds, surfaced in richly colored natural clay and capped with thatch held in place by pieces of bamboo.

Below left The entrance room and middle room of Shoiken (Laughing Mind Hut), divided by *fusuma* panels. The rear garden is visible through a large window, the lower sill of which is covered by a gilded velvet drape.

Below right A fence made of spicebush branches supported by horizontal bamboo poles extends from the Chumon (Central Gate), formerly known as the Onarikaya (Imperial Gate).

Shugakuin Imperial Villa

修学院離宮

LOCATION **SAKYO-KU**

ESTABLISHED IN **1659**

BUILT FOR **RETIRED EMPEROR GO-MIZUNOO**

Above Miyukimon (a gate for the exclusive use of the Emperor), the entrance to the Shimo no Ochaya (lower tea house) area.

Opposite above The path leading past Jugetsukan, the elegant villa in the Shimo no Ochaya area.

Opposite below left The villa is surrounded by a small garden containing a pond and stream fed by rainwater from Mount Hiei.

Opposite below right Built in the nineteenth century, this is a replica of the original Jugetsukan. The various paintings inside are attributed to the artists Kishi Ganku (1756–1839) and Okamoto Toyohiko (1773–1845).

Shugakuin Imperial Villa stands within the magnificent natural landscape of the foothills of the Higashiyama mountains, and was built as a retreat for Retired Emperor Go-Mizunoo (1596–1680). The site had been previously occupied by a Buddhist convent called Ensho-ji, in which Go-Mizunoo's eldest daughter, Bunchi, lived as a nun. Go-Mizunoo was so impressed by the surroundings that he had Ensho-ji and its inhabitants relocated to Nara Province in order to build the villa. The original buildings and gardens were probably designed by Go-Mizunoo himself—the apocryphal story is that he would give instructions to the artisans by disguising himself as a maidservant and traveling to the construction site in a palanquin.

Shugakuin Imperial Villa comprises three independent gardens set at different elevations on the slopes, linked by long paths lined with pine trees to screen them from the surrounding rice fields and farmers. These three areas are known as the Shimo no Ochaya (lower tea house), Naka no Ochaya (middle tea house), and Kami no Ochaya (upper tea house). Each contains one or two small *sukiya*-style pavilions. The upper garden is dominated by an artificial lake called Yokuryu-chi (Pond of the Bathing Dragon), overlooked by the Rin'untei (Pavilion Next to the Clouds). The two larger islands in the lake are linked by three bridges made of wood, earth, and stone respectively. The Kyusuitei (Distant Pavilion) located on one of the islands is the only original structure. The villa in the middle garden was originally built for Go-Mizunoo's eighth daughter, Genyo. After his death she became a nun and converted it into a temple called Rinkyu-ji. In 1885 this became part of Shugakuin Imperial Villa proper.

Forming an extensive, panoramic *kaiyushiki teien* (stroll garden), Shugakuin Imperial Villa has an equally spectacular backdrop. The design makes full use of *shakkei* (borrowed scenery), a Japanese landscape gardening technique that involves visually incorporating distant elements from the surrounding landscape while screening the immediate neighborhood from view. Mountains, forests, rice fields, and waterfalls are thus drawn into an extraordinarily beautiful and somewhat surreal microcosm.

Above left Built around 1668, Rakushiken was the original residence of Princess Genyo, the eighth daughter of Retired Emperor Go-Mizunoo.

Above center Flexible interior spaces at Rakushiken are enabled by sliding *fusuma* panels.

Above right The veranda around Kyakuden in the Naka no Ochaya area. Relocated from the Nyoin Palace in 1682, Kyakuden was used as a new residence by Princess Genyo.

Below The south face of Kyakuden. On the right a small flight of stone steps leads up the hill.

Right The image on the door inside Kyakuden depicts carp caught in a net. Visible beyond is the *kasumidana*, a famous set of decorative shelves made of zelkova wood.

Left The lawn on the west side of Rakushiken contains a *kasamatsu* (Japanese umbrella pine) trained on bamboo poles into a broad canopy shape.

Below The images on these *sugi* (Japanese cedar) doors inside the Kyakuden depict *hoko* (floats) used in the annual Gion Festival.

Above The interior of Kyusuitei (Pavilion in the Far Distance), the only building surviving from the original Shugakuin Imperial Villa.

Left A stone lantern in the Kami no Ochaya (upper tea house) garden.

Below An exterior view of Kyusuitei, which is located at the highest point of the main island in Yokuryu-chi (Pond of the Bathing Dragon).

Below Kaedebashi (Maple Tree Bridge) leading to the main island in Yokuryu-chi.

Right The view of the Kitayama hills beyond Kami no Ochaya from Rinuntei (Pavilion Next to the Clouds) is a fine example of *shakkei* (borrowed scenery).

Left The single room inside Kyusuitei is eighteen tatami mats in area. The six mats in the northwest corner, which are slightly raised and edged with a black-lacquered frame, are intended as a spot for sitting and observing the garden.

Kyoto Imperial Palace 京都御所

LOCATION **KAMIGYO-KU**

ESTABLISHED IN **1331**

BUILT FOR **EMPEROR KOGON**

Kyoto was the nominal capital of Japan for over a thousand years, but during much of that time effective power lay elsewhere. While the Imperial family lived in secluded irrelevance in their Kyoto palace, a series of samurai warlords fought for dominance over the nation. The Edo Period (1603–1868) saw Japan reunified in the wake of a century of devastating civil wars, with a military regime (the Tokugawa Shogunate) taking control and imposing peace, stability, and unity from their base in Edo, a coastal city located far to the east of Kyoto. The Emperor was finally restored to power in 1868, and the nation's capital officially relocated from Kyoto to Edo—the latter city was then renamed Tokyo. In 1869 the Imperial family moved to their new home in Tokyo, and many of the residences within the grounds of the old Imperial Palace (now known as the Kyoto Gosho) were demolished, but in 1877 Emperor Meiji (1852–1912) decreed that the remainder be preserved.

The original Imperial Palace, built for the founding of Heian-kyo in 794, was located southwest of the current location. The current palace location was originally one of several *satodairi* (temporary palaces) located throughout the city, and was first designated as the official palace in 1331 by Emperor Kogon (1313–64). The buildings themselves have been destroyed and rebuilt repeatedly, eight times during the Edo period alone, of which six were due to fire. Most of the current buildings date from 1855.

Enclosed by a thick clay wall, the palace grounds contain an array of independent structures that display the full range of Kyoto's traditional architectural styles. Seiryoden, the Imperial residence, and Shishinden, the ceremonial hall, are both built in the *shinden* style, with the *shoin* style represented by Otsunegoten, an annex to the main residence. A mixture of *shinden* and *shoin* styles is manifest in the Kogosho, a building used for official ceremonies. Constructed in 2005, the Geihinkan, or Kyoto State Guest House, is an outstanding example of modernized *sukiya* architecture.

Far left Kenreimon (named for Empress Dowager Kenrei), the south gate to the palace grounds, through which even today only the Emperor may pass.

Left Kenshunmon, the east gate, formerly used by the Empresses and Empress Dowagers.

Above A view from inside the palace compound, looking toward the Jomeimon gate, with the Kenreimon gate visible beyond.

Far left The central flight of steps leading up to the Shishinden is symbolically flanked by a mandarin tree and a cherry tree.

Left The view directly up the flight of steps leading to the Shishinden reveals the rich layers of brackets and purlins supporting the eaves.

Left The 1855 reconstruction of the Shishinden, as seen from between the vermillion columns of the Jomeimon gate. This is the main hall of the Kyoto Imperial Palace, still used for enthronement ceremonies and other major events.

Right The veranda of the *shinden*-style Seiryoden (Refreshing Hall), a building used as the private quarters of the Emperor until the mid-Heian Period (794–1185).

Above The north side of the Kogosho (Small Palace) faces onto an open courtyard once used for *kemari*, a type of football played by palace courtiers.

Below The east side of Giyoden antechamber, originally built to store the Emperor's valuables.

Far left A room inside the *shoin*-style Otsunegoten (Everyday Palace), the largest structure in the palace grounds. Built in the late Muromachi Period (1336–1573), it was used as the Emperor's residence until the capital shifted to Tokyo.

Left The roof gable of the Kogosho. Formerly used by the Emperor to receive important guests, the building was destroyed by fire in 1954 and rebuilt in 1958.

Below The corridor along the Higyosha (one of the five ladies' quarters), also known as Fujitsubo (Wisteria Court) because of the wisteria growing in its patio garden.

Above Okurumayose (carriage porch), where guests of the Imperial court would first arrive. Many were permitted to bring their ox carriages right into this space.

Left Oike-niwa (Pond Garden) is a landscaped stroll garden centered on a large pond. The pond contains a sandbar, stepping stones, bridges, small islands, and a boat dock.

Daikaku-ji 大覚寺

LOCATION **UKYO-KU**

ESTABLISHED IN **876**

BUILT FOR **EMPEROR SAGA**

Above Named Murasame-no-roka (Corridor of Passing Showers), this zigzag-shaped exterior corridor is intended to evoke the shape of a thunderbolt. All of the exterior veranda floors are constructed using a technique known as *uguisubari*, which causes them to sound like chirping birds when walked on.

Located in the Saga district on the northern outskirts of Kyoto, Daikaku-ji is a Buddhist temple that was once a detached palace known as Sagaso, the property of Emperor Saga (786–842). In 876 it was converted into a Buddhist temple by his daughter Empress Seishi (810–79). Her son, Prince Tsunesada (825–84), became the first abbot—Daikaku-ji is a *monzeki* temple, in which the abbots are always of imperial or aristocratic lineage. The temple adopted the doctrines of Shingon Buddhism, a sect founded by the monk Kukai (774–835). Also known as Kobo Daishi, Kukai had studied esoteric Buddhism in China, but upon returning to Japan earlier than expected found himself unwelcome in Kyoto. In 809 he was ordered to remain sequestered in a temple on Mount Takao, northwest of Kyoto. That same year Emperor Saga ascended to the throne and became a friend and supporter of Kukai, eventually returning him to public prominence.

Emperor Saga and his guests often went boating on Osawa-no-ike, the adjacent artificial lake. Its form was inspired by Lake Dongting in China's Hunan province, said to be the origin of dragon boating, and indeed dragon boating still takes place here today during the October moon-viewing parties. Thanks to Emperor Saga's cultural and aesthetic inclinations, Daikaku-ji has long been renowned as a site of cultural creativity as much as religious faith. He is said to have been the inventor of ikebana flower arrangement, and there is a prominent international ikebana school dedicated to his style, called Saga Goryu. Daikaku-ji was destroyed by fire in 1338 and rebuilt at a reduced size, then significantly altered in 1626 when Emperor Go-Mizunoo (1596–1680) relocated his own imperial hall of state to become the new main hall for the temple. Richly decorated, the temple still manifests the influence of *shinden*-style architecture and garden design.

Left Looking across the veranda of the Miedo hall, built in 1925. In the background is the Shinden, a building donated to the temple by Emperor Go-Mizunoo in 1626.

Below Looking across the central courtyard, with the Miedo on the left, the Godaido hall on the right, and the Goreiden hall in the middle.

Right The Botan-no-ma (Peony Room) of the Shinden, in which eighteen *fusuma* panels are covered with reproductions of paintings of peonies by Kano Sanraku (1559–1635).

Far left above Located in the Shinden, this Momoyama Period painting, called "Kohakubai-zu" (Red and White Plum Blossoms), is by Kano Sanraku (1559–1635).

Left above Also located in the Shinden, this is a detail of "Nosagizu" (Hares) by Shiko Watanabe (1683–1755). The full work depicts nineteen hares across twelve panels.

Left below The interior of the Shoshinden looking through to the Jodan-no-ma, the room from which Retired Emperor Go-Uda exercised clandestine political power.

Above A Saga Goryo-style ikebana flower arrangement set in the entry hall.

Left A view of the Osawa-no-ike pond from the moon-viewing platform of Godaido, the main temple at Daikaku-ji. This garden was commissioned by Emperor Saga with the intention of evoking Lake Dongting in China's Hunan Province.

Byodo-in 平等院

LOCATION **UJI**

BUILT IN **998**

BUILT FOR **FUJIWARA MICHINAGA**

Above The entrance gate to the Byodo-in precinct.

Opposite Looking south across Aji-ike pond toward the Amida Hall, popularly known as the Phoenix Hall. The central room houses a famed image of the Amida Buddha, surrounded by a frieze comprising fifty-two statues of bodhisattvas riding on clouds, each sculpted from a single piece of *hinoki* (Japanese cypress).

Byodo-in is located in Uji, a satellite city of Kyoto once famous as the locale of summer villas for the aristocracy. The setting for key scenes in *Genji Monogatari* (The Tale of Genji), a classic of Japanese literature, Byodo-in is now a functioning Buddhist temple jointly maintained by the Jodo and Tendai sects, but began life as a country villa belonging to nobleman Minamoto Toru, who in 998 gave it to Fujiwara Michinaga (966–1028), de facto ruler of Japan in the early eleventh century. In 1052 it was converted to a Buddhist temple by his son, Fujiwara Yorimichi, and the following year the Phoenix Hall (also known as the Amida Hall) was built—the only structure to have survived the fires of civil war in 1336, and still held in such high regard that it appears on the modern 10 yen coin.

Surrounded by an artificial pond, the Phoenix Hall comprises a central hall symmetrically flanked by corridors on either side and one to the rear; the name derives from the resemblance of this arrangement to two outstretched wings and a tail, echoed by the Chinese phoenix statues adorning the roof. Other elements, including the subtle curvature at the ends of the eaves, not to mention the striking symmetry of the overall composition, reflect a strong Chinese influence on the architecture. The central hall houses an image of Amida Buddha intended to be visible from the opposite side of the pond, which is itself designed to evoke the sacred lake of Jodo Buddhism, where saved souls sit in eternal rapture on floating lotus leaves.

Completed in 2000, the Byodo-in Museum is located within the temple grounds and houses the temple's most valuable artifacts. In direct contrast with the Phoenix Hall's monumental symmetry, the museum is a sophisticated work of restrained Japanese modern architecture, comprising a partly underground, asymmetrically meandering route.

Left Jodo-in (Pure Land Hall), a *tatchu* (subtemple) of Byodo-in, established in the late fifteenth century.

Right The broad veranda of Jodo-in.

Below left Rakando (Hexagonal Hall), built in 1640.

Below The offering box located in front of Jodo-in.

Opposite below left An elaborate *ranma* (open lintel) in Saisho-in, the other subtemple of Byodo-in.

Opposite below center A detail of the shoji screens in Jodo-in.

Opposite below right A phoenix sculpture on the roof of the Phoenix Hall. This is a replica of the original, which is on display in the nearby Byodo-in Museum.

Right The Golden Pavilion is situated on the north side of the Kyoko-chi (Mirror Pond), and reflected in its waters.

Opposite The lower level, known as Hosuiin (Chamber of Dharma Waters), has been designed in *shinden* style. The middle level, known as Choondo (Hall of Roaring Waves), is in *buke zukuri*, the so-called samurai style. The upper-level cupola, known as Kukyocho (Firmament Top), is in the Sung Dynasty Chinese-influenced style known as *karayo*.

Kinkaku-ji 金閣寺

LOCATION **KITA-KU**

ESTABLISHED IN **1397**

BUILT FOR **ASHIKAGA YOSHIMITSU**

The Rinzai Zen Buddhist temple Rokuon-ji, popularly known as Kinkaku-ji (the Temple of the Golden Pavilion), lies on the western edge of Kyoto against a spectacular backdrop of mountains. During the Kamakura Period (1185–1333), this area belonged to the aristocrat Saionji Kintsune (1171–1244), and contained a *shinden*-style villa as well as the Saion-ji family temple. When the Kamakura Shogunate collapsed, so too did the status of the Saionji family. The villa was abandoned, and the land appropriated by the third Ashikaga Shogun, Yoshimitsu (1358–1408), as the site for his retirement villa.

Under Yoshimitsu's patronage of the arts, the estate became the heart of so-called *kitayama bunka* (north mountain culture), which nurtured artistic pursuits such as *no* drama and *renga* linked verse, and was instrumental in introducing aspects of Ming Dynasty Chinese culture to Japan. Yoshimitsu originally constructed Kinkaku (the Golden Pavilion itself) as a *shariden* (Buddhist relic hall). A pioneering example of multistory construction in an era when almost every building in Japan had only a single story, the pavilion is partly clad in gold leaf, a surprisingly ostentatious gesture given the tradition of understatement that characterizes Kyoto. One explanation is that Yoshimitsu was attempting to impress the gold-loving Chinese, with whom he had been actively cultivating trading relationships. A more generous theory is that the gold is intended as a metaphorical reference to Buddhist scripture. Indeed, the effect is otherworldly: set adjacent to the Kyoko-ike (Mirror Pond), many observers have asserted that the pavilion is best appreciated by looking at its reflection rather than the building itself. Similar to Byodo-in temple, the composition of pavilion and pond recalls descriptions of the Amida Buddha's paradise in Jodo Buddhism. Upon Yoshimitsu's death, the estate was turned into a temple, with Muso Soseki (1275–1351) as its first abbot. The present Kinkaku dates from 1955, following its complete destruction by arson in 1950, the act of a deranged acolyte then living at the temple.

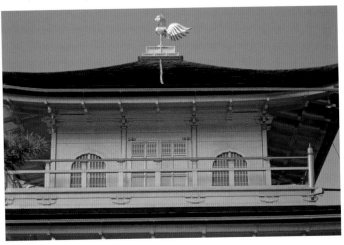

Above As part of a typical *shinden*-style estate, the pond would have been located south of the villa and used for boating parties.

Left Also clad in gold leaf, the bronze statue of a phoenix on the roof of the Golden Pavilion is over a meter in height.

Right A small pavilion selling *omamori* (amulets) to visitors.

Below The *hojo* (abbot's quarters).

夕佳亭

Above The distinctive *tokobashira* post in the *tokonoma* alcove of Sekkatei is made of nandina wood, commonly known as sacred bamboo (though it is not actually a type of bamboo).

Right Designed by influential tea master Kanamori Sowa (1548–1656), Sekkatei (Pleasant Evening Pavilion) is a *sukiya*-style tea house originally built in anticipation of a visit by Emperor Go-Mizunoo. It was destroyed by fire in 1874 and reconstructed in 1884.

Far right The long path of gentle steps leading out of the temple precinct.

Below left Moss growing on the revetment of the clay wall at the perimeter of the temple precinct.

Below right Moss growing on the thatched roof of Sekkatei.

Ginkaku-ji 銀閣寺

LOCATION **SAKYO-KU**

ESTABLISHED IN **1490**

BUILT FOR **ASHIKAGA YOSHIMASA**

Above The stone path leading to the Somon (entrance gate).

Opposite The first floor of the Silver Pavilion, known as Shinkuden (Empty Heart Hall), is in *shoin* style, and the second floor, known as Choonkaku (Pavilion of Roaring Waves), is in a Chinese-influenced style with distinctive *katomado* (lantern-shaped windows). A phoenix sculpture sits at the peak of the pyramid-shaped roof.

At the age of eight, Ashikaga Yoshimasa (1436–1490) was appointed Shogun, nominal leader of a nation being torn apart by civil strife. An inept politician but born aesthete, Yoshimasa's reign culminated in the Onin War (1467–77)—the outbreak of which was triggered partly by his own actions—leading to the destruction of most of Kyoto. In 1473, with the city in flames, Yoshimasa decided to retire and devote his time to artistic pursuits. Jodo-ji, a temple located in the Higashiyama foothills at the edge of the city, had been razed at the outset of the war and Yoshimasa decided it would be an ideal location for his retirement villa. Under his influence and patronage, Kyoto went on to experience a period of extraordinary artistic development, collectively known as *higashiyama bunka* (east mountain culture). Yoshimasa ordered the formalization of *shoin*-style architecture and initiated the tradition of Daimon-ji, an annual festival in which enormous ideograms are delineated with bonfires on five mountainsides around the city.

As per Yoshimasa's instructions, the villa was converted to a Rinzai Zen Buddhist temple after his death. Now officially called Tozan Jisho-ji, most of the temple buildings were destroyed in 1550 and rebuilt in the early seventeenth century, but two structures survive more or less intact from the original villa. One is Togudo (Hall of the Eastern Quest), which contains the earliest known *yojohan* (four and a half tatami mat) tea ceremony room. The other is the Kannon Hall, which Yoshimasa modeled on Kinkaku (the Golden Pavilion) built by his grandfather, Shogun Ashikaga Yoshimitsu (1358–1408). Although it was never clad with silver leaf, the hall later became popularly known as Ginkaku (the Silver Pavilion) and the entire temple as Gingaku-ji. Similar to Kinkaku, the upper level of Gingaku was designed in the Chinese Zen style, and the lower level in the *shinden* style, although the original *shitomido* (exterior wooden panels) have been replaced with shoji screens

Above left The building to the rear is Togudo, a Buddhist hall built in 1486. This structure contains the earliest extant example of a *yojohan* (four and a half tatami mat) room. Called Dojinsai, it was Yoshimasa's study, and designed by his tea advisor Murata Shuko (1423–1503).

Above right Ginshadan (Sea of Silver Sand), a plateau of raked white gravel, set in clear contrast to the naturalistic composition of the adjacent garden.

Left The entrance to the *kuri* (priests' quarters).

Left Kogetsudai (Platform Facing the Moon), a truncated cone of white gravel said to evoke Mount Fuji.

Below An elevated view of Ginshadan and Kogetsudai, located northeast of the Silver Pavilion. The building on the right is the *hondo* (main hall), which dates to the mid-Edo Period (1603–1868).

Jakko-in 寂光院

LOCATION **SAKYO-KU**

ESTABLISHED IN **594**

BUILT FOR **CROWN PRINCE SHOTOKU**

The life story of Taira Tokuko (1155–1213) reappears throughout Japanese literature, most notably in the *Heike Monogatari* (The Tale of the Heike), an epic account of the struggle between the Taira and Minamoto clans for control of the Imperial court. At the age of seventeen, Tokuko became a consort of her first cousin, Emperor Takakura, who was then aged eleven. Takakura abdicated in 1180, and their two-year-old child Tokihito (1178–85) was enthroned, taking the name Emperor Antoku. Tokuko then became known as Kenreimon'in (Empress Dowager Kenrei). That year also saw the beginning of the Genpei War, the culmination of the conflict between the Taira and the Minamoto. In 1185 the war (and the Heian Period itself) ended with the overwhelming defeat of the Taira in a sea battle. Victims of treachery, the Taira warriors committed suicide rather than live with the shame. Taira Tokiko, matriarch of the clan, drowned herself with her grandson, the eight-year-old Emperor Antoku, clasped in her arms. Kenreimon'in tried to follow, but was saved from the waves by the enemy; it was customary for the victors to keep a single survivor so that they may pray for their own dead. That year, she became a Buddhist nun and was permitted to take up residence at Jakko-in, a convent in the village of Ohara, northeast of Kyoto. She remained there in melancholy seclusion until her death.

Jakko-in is one of the oldest temples in Japan: it was reputedly established by Crown Prince Shotoku (574–622) as a memorial to his father, Emperor Yomei (540–87). Toyotomi Hideyori (1593–1615), son and successor of Hideyoshi, restored the buildings and garden in the early seventeenth century. The exquisite garden contains two small ponds connected by a stream running directly in front of the *hondo* (main hall). Destroyed by arson in 2000, the *hondo* was rebuilt by 2005. Also ruined in the fire was a famed wooden statue of the bodhisattva Jizo (protector of children), to which Kenreimon'in prayed in memory of her son, but this has since been replicated.

Above The tip of the eaves among the foliage.

Opposite above The *hondo* (main hall), rebuilt in 2005 following its destruction by fire in 2000. It contains a statue of the bodhisattva Jizo as well as a figurine of Kenreimon'in.

Opposite below left The stone staircase leading to the entrance gate, through which the roof of the *hondo* is partly visible.

Opposite below right Largely concealed by plants and stones, a stream connecting the two ponds in the garden runs in front of the temple.

Right The temple belfry.

Below Connected to the *hondo* by a roofed walkway, the building on the right is the Shoin, said to be where Kenreimon'in lived. The iron lantern set in front of the walkway was bequeathed to the temple by Toyotomi Hideyori (1593–1615).

Right The façade of the Shoin, beyond which lies the larger of the two ponds.

Below left A small tea house is located slightly further down the slope, accessible directly from the main stair leading to the temple gate.

Below right Gray roof tiles amid autumn foliage.

temple residences

The residence of the abbot in a Zen Buddhist temple or monastery is called a *hojo*, which literally means a square area of one *jo* per side (in the traditional Japanese measurement system, one *jo* equals about 3 meters), enough to contain about four and a half tatami mats. The name is said to be a symbolic reference to the size of the stone chamber of Vimalakirti, the "enlightened layman" of Mahayana Buddhism. The most famous *hojo* in Kyoto's history was a mountain hut built at the beginning of the thirteenth century by Kamo no Chomei (1155–1216), an aristocrat, scholar, and late-life convert to Buddhism. Having witnessed the many traumatic events that occurred in Kyoto during the transition from the Heian Period to the Kamakura Period—devastating fires, storms, and earthquakes, extended periods of famine and civil war—Chomei retreated to the foothills of Mount Hino, southeast of the city. There he built himself a small, fragile hut in which to live out the remainder of his life in peace, studying the Buddhist scriptures, playing music, and writing poetry. He describes his dwelling and lifestyle in an essay or letter titled *Hojoki* (generally translated as *The Ten Foot Square Hut*), one of the most famous works of Japanese literature. Taking transience as its theme, the text is a Buddhism-inspired treatise on human vanity and material impermanence.

As living quarters for abbots, most *hojo* are larger and more substantial than this (indeed, Chomei's hut is one of the key inspirations for the rustic tea house style known as *soan chashitsu*), but all retain a profound sense of ascetic and aesthetic devotion to Buddhist principles. From the middle of the Muromachi Period (1333–1573) onward, the *hojo* was often used as the temple's *hondo* (main hall), housing Buddhist icons and statues of the founding priest. Larger temple compounds will also contain subtemples called *tatchu*, which are initially built as either living quarters for retired abbots or as memorial temples to deceased ones. These subtemples tend to include repositories for valuable artifacts and graveyards for important historical figures.

Ryogen-in 大徳寺 龍源院

LOCATION **KITA-KU**

BUILT IN **1502**

ORIGINAL OWNER **TOKEI SOBOKU**

Founded in 1502 as a residence for Daitoku-ji's seventy-second abbot, Tokei Soboku (1455–1517), Ryogen-in is a *tatchu* (subtemple) of the Daitoku-ji complex. The *hojo* of Ryogen-in, a single-story building with an *irimoya* (hipped and gabled) roof, dates from around 1517, making it one of the oldest extant examples of this type of architecture. Ryogen-in contains several superb examples of *karesansui* (dry landscape) garden design, a style that reached its apogee during the Muromachi Period (1336–1568). The *hojo* is surrounded by five independent gardens. To the south is a stone garden called Isshidan, which contains rock formations intended to represent a crane, a tortoise, and Mount Shumisen (the mountain at the center of the universe, according to traditional Buddhist cosmology). The circular island of moss was created by the present abbot, Katsudo Hosoai, to replace an ancient camellia tree that died in 1980. To the west is a small moss garden called Keizokusan, and to the north is a larger rectangular moss garden called Ryugintei, generally attributed to the famous artist and aesthete Soami (1472–1525) and unchanged since the founding of the temple. Contained between the *kuri* (priests' quarters) and the east side of the *hojo* is Totekiko, the smallest stone garden in Japan, its concentric rings of raked gravel around the stones intended to represent water ripples. This garden was created in 1960 by Nabeshima Gakusho (1913–69), one of the most talented pupils of famed garden designer Shigemori Mirei (1896–1975); Nabeshima was the chief assistant for the latter's nationwide documentation of historical garden designs, which he distilled into the flawless composition of Totekiko. Southeast of the *hojo* is Kodatei, also known as the "a-un" garden. Symbolizing the creativity of cosmic opposites—inhaling and exhaling, heaven and earth, male and female—these syllables are represented by two stones that were salvaged from the foundations of Jurakudai, an ostentatious palace belonging to Toyotomi Hideyoshi (1536–98), which was completed in 1588 but dismantled less than a decade later.

Previous spread Enclosed garden at Kanchi-in.

Above The path leading to the entrance hall and *kuri* (priests' quarters).

Opposite A view of the Isshidan garden from the northwest corner. To the right is the *hojo*, the oldest surviving example of this architectural type. The large island of moss in the foreground was created in 1980 to replace an ancient camellia tree.

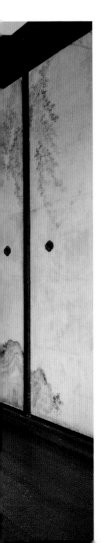

Far left The cluster of stones at the east end of Isshidan is thought to represent Mount Shumisen, the mythical mountain at the center of the universe according to traditional Buddhist cosmology.

Center left In keeping with the name of the temple (which means "origin of the dragon") the *fusuma* panels in the middle room of the *hojo* are decorated with a powerful image of a dragon by an unknown artist.

Left A plaque hanging above a finely latticed window in the *hojo*.

Below left The middle room of the *hojo* is an *itanoma*—floored with wooden boards rather than tatami mats.

Above Located on the north side of the *hojo*, Ryugintei is the oldest of the five gardens at Ryogen-in and is attributed to the painter Soami (1472–1525). Now covered in moss, the garden was originally an expanse of gravel.

Left Kaisodo, the founder's hall, is a single-story, Chinese-influenced structure with an *irimoya* (hipped and gabled) roof clad in cypress bark.

Below As in the Isshidan garden, the tallest stone in Ryugintei is thought to represent Mount Shumisen.

Shoren-in 青蓮院門跡

LOCATION **HIGASHIYAMA-KU**

ESTABLISHED IN **1144**

ORIGINAL OWNER **GYOGEN**

Above A path through the Soami-no-niwa.

Opposite The Shinden was relocated here from the Imperial Palace during the eighteenth century, and used as a temporary palace by Retired Empress Go-Sakuramachi. This is a reconstruction following a fire in 1893.

Shoren-in was first established as a new home for Gyogen (1093–1152), the forty-eighth abbot of Enryaku-ji, a huge Tendai Buddhist temple complex located on Mount Hiei. Retired Emperor Toba (1103–56) assigned his seventh son, Prince Kakukai, to be a student of Gyogen, and built Shoren-in in the Higashiyama district of Kyoto in 1144. Fear of floods later caused a move to higher ground at the foot of Mount Awata, and the *shinden*-style building became commonly known as the Awata Palace. Prince Kakukai was appointed the second abbot of Shoren-in in 1155, initiating the *monzeki* tradition in which successive abbots were all members of the nobility or aristocracy. Shoren-in is the most important of the five *monzeki* temples in Kyoto, although the tradition ended with the beginning of the Meiji Period (1868–1912) and the concomitant government suppression of Buddhism.

The original Shinden was destroyed in the Onin War (1467–77), but was quickly rebuilt. When Tokugawa Masako (1607–78), daughter of Shogun Tokugawa Hidetata (1579–1632), became a consort to Emperor Go-Mizunoo (1596–1680), a residence was built for her in the Imperial Palace precinct and portions of it were later dismantled and distributed among various temples. The main building became the new Shinden of Shoren-in, and following the 1788 Temmei fire, which devastated Kyoto, it was used as a temporary palace by Retired Empress Go-Sakuramachi (1740–1813). The garden *chashitsu* Kobuntei was destroyed by arson in 1993, but its original Edo Period form has been accurately replicated, right down to the exact types of wood; the new building was inaugurated by Sen Soshitsu, current head of the Urasenke tea school. The extraordinary *chisenkaiyushiki teien* (pond stroll garden) has its origins in the Muromachi Period (1336–1573), and is usually attributed to the artist and aesthete Soami (1472–1525), although it was rebuilt in the early twentieth century by Ogawa Jihei (1860–1933). North of Kobuntei is the flower-covered Garden of Kirishima, attributed to tea master Kobori Enshu (1579–1647).

Left and below left
Images of *hoko* (floats) painted on a door in the Kogosho, a building formerly used as the residence of the abbot.

Bottom A large room in the Shinden, adjoining a sheltered *engawa*.

Opposite above A room inside the Kachoden, with framed pictures of thirty-six famous poets on display above the *fusuma* panels. The images of lotus flowers on the *fusuma* were added in 2005, and are the work of contemporary artist Kimura Hideki (1942–).

Opposite below left A superb example of antique furniture on display in the entry hall.

Opposite below right A detail of one of the sixty *fusuma* panels by Kimura Hideki in the Kachoden.

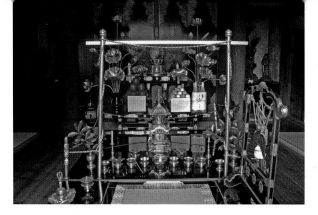

Left A view of the Kacho-den from the Soami-no-niwa garden.

Below A stone bridge crossing the Ryushin-no-ike (Dragon Heart Pond) in the Soami-no-niwa, a garden attributed to Soami (1472–1525).

Opposite above left Buddhist offerings on display.

Left A *tokonoma* alcove inside the Kachoden reception hall.

Opposite above right Two *butsudan* (altars) containing *gohonzon* (representations of the Buddha, or of Buddhist deities)

Tofuku-ji 東福寺

LOCATION **HIGASHIYAMA-KU**

ESTABLISHED IN **1236**

BUILT FOR **KUJO MICHIIE**

Tofuku-ji is a Rinzai Zen Buddhist temple established in 1236 for the monk Enni Ben'en (1202–80) at the order of Kujo Michiie (1193–1252), a *kampaku* (senior advisor to the Emperor) during the Kamakura Period (1185–1333). The original buildings have been lost to fire and war, though the temple was rebuilt during the fifteenth century in a layout close to the original.

The current *hojo* (main hall) is a reconstruction dating from 1890. In 1938 the head priest invited a little-known garden designer called Shigemori Mirei (1896–1975) to produce a scheme for the long-term improvement of the entire temple precinct. Mirei's first step was to design new gardens for all four sides of the *hojo*, which he completed the following year. The temple had little money for the project, so Mirei worked for free. In keeping with the Zen proscription against wastage, he was asked to make use of old construction materials lying around the temple grounds.

Nevertheless, this was the commission that made Mirei famous. The four extraordinary gardens he created are known collectively as the Hasso-no-niwa (Garden of Eight Views). The southern garden comprises four rock clusters symbolizing the mythical Islands of the Immortals on a white sand surface representing the sea, and five moss-covered mounds representing sacred mountains set on a triangular field of moss in the west corner. The western garden is composed of azaleas trimmed into squares and arrayed in a checkerboard pattern. The eastern garden is a cloud-shaped field of gravel surrounded by moss, containing seven cylindrical stones (foundation piles salvaged from an outhouse elsewhere on the temple grounds) arranged to represent the stars of the Big Dipper. Yet, it is the northern garden—a checkerboard pattern of leftover paving stones set into moss, the regular grid dissolving away from west to east—that caused the most controversy. Then seen as iconoclastic, it has since become one of the iconic images of Japanese garden design.

Above left A detail of the elegantly intersecting hand-rails on the veranda overlooking the south garden.

Above right Set across a triangular patch of moss, the five mounds in the west corner of the south garden represent sacred mountains.

Left A detail of the four rock clusters in the south garden.

Left The eastern garden is a cloud-shaped field of gravel surrounded by moss, containing seven cylindrical stones arranged to represent the stars of the Big Dipper.

Below The northern garden is a checkerboard pattern of leftover paving stones set into moss, the regular grid dissolving away from west to east.

Opposite above The west garden (Ryu-no-niwa) is intended to represent a dragon ascending from the sea to heaven through a storm. Geometric patterns on the bamboo fence symbolize flashes of lightning.

Opposite below left The south garden (Mu-no-niwa) is a simple expanse of white sand.

Opposite below right The approach path to Ryogin-an.

Ryogin-an 東福寺 龍吟庵

LOCATION **HIGASHIYAMA-KU**

ESTABLISHED IN **1291**

BUILT FOR **MUKAN FUMON**

Located within the grounds of Tofuku-ji temple, Ryogin-an was originally the residence of Mukan Fumon (1212–91), the temple's third abbot. Upon his death, the house was converted into Tofuku-ji's first *tatchu* (subtemple). The *hojo* (abbot's quarters) of Ryogin-an is believed to have been built in 1387, making it the oldest extant example of this type of architecture. It is now an officially designated National Treasure and opened to the public in November every year. Elements such as the hinged double-door of the front entrance and the *yarido* wooden shutters inserted either side reveal traces of the *shinden* style within this *shoin*-style building. Located to the rear of the *hojo* is the temple hall, where a statue of Fumon is enshrined.

There are three gardens adjacent to the *hojo*, along the east, west, and south sides. They are all *karesansui* (dry landscape) gardens, evocative compositions comprising rocks and gravel of various hues, designed by Shigemori Mirei (1896–1975) and completed in 1964. The south garden, Mu-no-niwa (Garden of Nothingness), set at the front face of the *hojo*, is a simple expanse of white sand. The arrangement of stones set in the reddish granite gravel of the east garden, Furi-no-niwa (Garden of Inseparability), is inspired by a tale from Fumon's childhood: while wandering alone and ill in the mountains he was attacked by a wolf, but two dogs came to his rescue. Echoing the name of the temple (*ryogin* means "chanting dragon"), the west garden, Ryumon-no-niwa (Dragon Gate Garden), is intended to represent a dragon ascending from the sea to heaven through a storm. A curving line of independent stones represents the dragon's body, twisting through cloud shapes delineated in white and gray sand, with a larger cluster of stones as its head. The design is said to give the illusion of movement as one walks along the west face of the *hojo*.

Above The arrangement of stones in the east garden (Furi-no-niwa) is inspired by a tale from Fumon's childhood: while wandering alone and ill in the mountains, he was attacked by a wolf, but two dogs came to his rescue.

Ninna-ji 仁和寺

LOCATION **UKYO-KU**

ESTABLISHED IN **888**

BUILT FOR **EMPEROR UDA**

Appropriating a site on the west side of Kyoto that formerly contained a summer villa belonging to the Imperial family, in 886 Emperor Koko (830–87) established a Shingon Buddhist temple called Nishiyama Gogan-ji. He died soon afterward and the completion of construction was supervised by his successor, Emperor Uda (867–931), who renamed it Ninna-ji. Uda retired in 897 and moved into Ninna-ji in 900, building himself a residence within the temple grounds called the Omuro Palace. He was the temple's first *monzeki* (abbot of Imperial lineage), a position he held for thirty years before being succeeded by one of his sons. From then onward, the reigning Emperor would send a son to take over the role of head priest when the previous one died, a practice discontinued at the beginning of the Meiji Period (1868–1912). During the Showa Period (1926–89), Ninna-ji became head temple of the Omuro school of Shingon Buddhism and home to the Omuro School of ikebana. In 1994 it was selected as one of Kyoto's numerous UNESCO-designated world heritage sites.

There was a significant pause in this venerable history: Ninna-ji was completely destroyed during the Onin War (1467–77), and for the next 150 years the *hoto* (Buddhist scripture) was preserved in a small building on Narabiga-oka, a hill just south of the vacant temple site. The temple complex was rebuilt in the 1630s under the patronage of Shogun Tokugawa Iemitsu (1604–51), adopting a layout close to the one that exists today. Iemitsu relocated and reassembled old structures from the Imperial Palace to become Ninna-ji's new *hondo* (main hall), *miedo* (founder's hall), and Omuro Palace. In 1887 many of the buildings were again destroyed by fire. An authentic *shinden*-style reconstruction of the Omuro Palace was completed in 1915. The vast temple precinct now contains a large and varied collection of buildings and gardens, including the seventeenth-century tea houses Ryokaku-tei and Hito-tei, a five-story pagoda, and a grove of cherry blossom trees.

Opposite A detail of the *engawa* running along the exterior perimeter of the Shinden, the main hall of the Omuro Palace. This building is a replica constructed in 1913, after the original was destroyed by fire.

Above A view of the main garden, located north of the Shinden—an orderly field of raked gravel meeting a freeform pond. The Hitotei tea house may be glimpsed among the trees, and the 36-meter-high *gojunoto* (five-storied pagoda) is visible beyond.

Below The gravel surface of the garden to the south of the Shinden.

Top left A distant view of the magnificent Niomon (Two Kings Gate) at the entry, believed to have been donated by the third Tokugawa Shogun, Iemitsu (1604–51).

Top right Built in the early seventeenth century, the *shinden*-style *kondo* (Buddhist Hall) was originally the Shishinden (Coronation Hall) of the Imperial Palace, later dismantled and relocated to Ninna-ji.

Above Decorated fusuma panels inside the Shiroshoin, a hall located adjacent to the Shinden.

Right A peripheral corridor in the Shinden, showing the subtle layering of spaces between the exterior and interior of the building.

Left The finely detailed shoji doors in the Shinden.

Below The *engawa* of the Shinden. Outdoor corridors link many of the buildings.

Above An ornate room inside the Shinden, containing characteristic elements of *shoin*-style architecture. The images on the walls and *fusuma* were painted by famed *nihonga* artist Hara Zaisen (1849–1916).

Nanzen-ji 南禅寺

LOCATION **SAKYO-KU**

BUILT IN **1264**

ORIGINAL OWNER **RETIRED EMPEROR GO-SAGA**

Above Sanmon (Mountain Gate) at the entrance to the temple grounds.

Opposite above The *honbo* (main residence) comprises two linked halls, the Ohojo (large hall) and Kohojo (small hall). The former was once part of the Kyoto Imperial Palace, and the latter was once part of Fushimi Castle.

Opposite below left Daigen gate, with its unusual *karahafu* (cusped gable) roof.

Opposite below right The facade of the *hondo* (main hall).

In 1264 Retired Emperor Go-Saga (1220–72) built an Imperial villa called Zenrinji-den at the foot of the Higashiyama mountains. Go-Saga's son and successor, Emperor Kameyama (1249–1305), ascended the throne at the age of ten, then retired in 1274 and took possession of his father's villa. Having become a Buddhist priest, he converted the villa to a temple in 1291, naming it Ryoanzan Zenrinzen-ji and appointing Mukan Fumon (1212–91) of Tofuku-ji temple as the head abbot. According to legend, Fumon and his acolytes had impressed Kameyama by exorcizing ghosts from the villa simply through Zen meditation. Sadly, Fumon died that same year and it was the second abbot, Kian Soen (1261–1313), who supervised the construction of the Nanzen-in subtemple that eventually gave Nanzen-ji its name. It was largely complete in 1305, the year of Kameyama's death, and the garden contains his mausoleum.

As Nanzen-ji's prestige and political power increased, boosted by the endorsement of Shogun Ashikaga Yoshimitsu (1358–1408), there was also a growing antagonism with the Enryaku-ji temple complex on Mount Hiei. This culminated in 1393 when the monks of Enryaku-ji attacked and torched Nanzen-ji. In 1447 it was again damaged by fire and quickly rebuilt, but suffered almost total destruction during the Onin War (1467–77). Nanzen-ji underwent a spectacular rebirth in the Edo Period (1603–1868), growing to become a vast estate with sixty-two subtemples, but most of this property was confiscated after the Meiji Restoration in 1868. As Kyoto began to implement modernization projects over the next few decades, a canal was built from Lake Biwa, in neighboring Shiga Prefecture, to Kyoto, passing through the grounds of Nanzen-ji across a Roman-style red brick aqueduct. This project drew public protests when first proposed but it is now comfortably ensconced as part of Nanzen-ji's historical legacy. Likewise, the extensive temple complex unobtrusively blends in with the surrounding neighborhood.

Left Stones, shrubs, and moss against a bamboo fence.

Below left to right A white plastered wall set as a backdrop to the Rokudotei moss garden; a stone set amid gravel, raked to evoke an island in the sea; a stone set on moss.

Above The many spectacular paintings on the gilded fusuma panels at Nanzen-ji are the work of Kano Tan'yu (1602–74), Kano Eitoku (1543–90), and Kano Motonobu (1476–1559), all members of the highly influential Kano school of painting.

Right A *tokonoma* alcove in the Shoin, softly lit by daylight filtered through the translucent shoji panels in the window.

Left Attributed to Kobori Enshu (1594–1634), the *karesansui* (dry landscape) garden adjacent to the Ohojo incorporates the Higashiyama mountains as borrowed scenery.

Below Nyoshintei, the austere *karesansui* garden adjacent to the Kohojo.

Above left Fushikian tea house glimpsed through foliage.

Above right A path leading to the Fushikian tea house.

Right The Hatto (lecture hall) was built in 1909, after the previous building was lost to fire in 1895.

Kanchi-in 東寺 観智院

LOCATION **MINAMI-KU**

BUILT IN **1308**

BUILT FOR **EMPEROR GO-UDA**

The first and the most prestigious *tatchu* (subtemple) of To-ji temple, Kanchi-in has been the residence of many generations of scholarly priests. Construction was begun in 1308 on the orders of Retired Emperor Go-Uda (1267–1324), and in 1359 it became an institute for the study of Shingon Buddhism. Kanchi-in is today home to one of the largest and best collections of Buddhist scriptures in Japan, comprising more than 15,000 sacred texts.

In 823 Kukai (774–835), also known as Kobo Daishi, was placed in charge of To-ji temple by Emperor Saga. Kukai had previously studied in China (supposedly his trip was inspired by a vision of Kokuzo, the Bodhisattva of All-Encompassing Wisdom), and the *karesansui* garden in front of the Kanchi-in reception hall tells the story of Kukai's journey home. The right-hand mound represents China, and the stones in the central area of gravel symbolize his boat and the three sea gods that protected him. The left-hand mound represents Japan, set within which are five stones corresponding to the Godai Kokuzo (five manifestations of Kokuzo). Statues of the Godai Kokuzo are also enshrined in the *butsuden* (Buddha hall) to the rear of the reception hall, each set on a *chojuza* (animal-shaped pedestal): lion, elephant, horse, peacock, and the mythical Garuda. These statues were brought over from Qinglong Temple in China's capital, Chang'an, in 847 and enshrined at Kanchi-in in 1376.

The reception hall itself was destroyed by an earthquake in 1596 and rebuilt in 1605 with the sponsorship of Hideyoshi's widow, Nene (1546–1624). It is a *shoin*-style building with characteristic elements such as a *tokonoma* and *chigaidana* in the main room, and a *tsukeshoin* and *chodaigamae* (decorative doors) in the living room. The reception hall also contains several paintings attributed to the famed samurai warrior Miyamoto Musashi (1584–1645), including a *fusuma* decorated with an image of a bamboo thicket that appears to have been painted with both hands, evoking his legendary ability to fight using two swords.

Top Kitamon (North Gate), with the roof of the reception hall visible on the right.

Above The enclosed space of the Shiho-shomen-no-niwa (Garden with Four Frontages).

Opposite An elevated, sheltered walkway extends from the Shoin across the Shihoshomen-no-niwa.

Below The *sukiya*-style interior of Fusenkan (Maple Fountain View), a *chashitsu* located north of the *butsuden* (Buddha hall). The vertically sliding shoji on the right are known as *yukimishoji* (snow-viewing screens), designed to suit the sightlines of people sitting on the floor.

Right The tea garden outside Fusenkan.

Right A *tokonoma* alcove inside Fusenkan—a rich, complex composition of subtle misalignments. The tea garden is visible through the adjacent opening.

Below left A *chozubachi* (stone bowl for wetting one's hands) located in the tea garden, filled by water flowing through a short bamboo rod.

Below center A detail of the courtyard garden, with a stone for placing shoes set next to the *engawa*.

Below right Godai-no-niwa, a *karesansui* (dry landscape) garden in which the composition of stones is based on a mythologized narrative of Kukai's journey home from China.

Jingo-ji 高雄山 神護寺

LOCATION **UKYO-KU**

ESTABLISHED IN **824**

BUILT FOR **WAKE KIYOMARO**

Above The steep flight of steps of rough-hewn stone leading up to the Romon (Tower Gate) entrance to the temple precinct.

Opposite A view from above, with the Godaido (Hall of the Five Great Deities) on the left and the Bishamondo hall on the right. Both buildings date from the 1623 reconstruction commissioned by Itakura Katsushige (1545–1624), a senior official in the Tokugawa Shogunate.

Poet, artist, calligrapher, and engineer, the monk Kukai (774–835) was the founder of Shingon Buddhism and one of the most influential figures in Kyoto's cultural history. He is commonly known by his posthumous name, Kobo Daishi. As a young prodigy searching for a way to unify the cerebral theories and visceral experiences of disparate Buddhist doctrines, Kukai eventually gained permission to join an official government trip to China in 804, on the condition that he stay there studying for twenty years. At Qinglong Temple, Kukai met the Chinese monk Hui-kuo (746–805), who began training him in esoteric Buddhism. Hui-kuo died within a few months, but not before anointing Kukai as his successor and instructing him to spread his teachings in Japan. Returning to Japan after only two years, Kukai initially found himself unwelcome in Kyoto, and in 809 he was ordered by the Emperor to reside in Takaosan-ji, a temple on Mount Takao located northwest of the city. He stayed there for the next fourteen years. In 824 Takaosan-ji was merged with the temple Jingan-ji, then located in Bizen Province (present-day Okayama), to become Jingo-ji, with Kukai appointed as the head priest and the temple dedicated to Shingon Buddhism. Both of the predecessor temples were founded by Wake Kiyomaro (733–99), an early sponsor of Buddhism and a close advisor to Emperor Kammu. Kiyomaro was instrumental in convincing Kammu to abandon the previous capital Nagaoka-kyo and shift to the site of what was to become Kyoto. Jingo-ji is Kiyomaro's family temple, and he is interred here.

The temple has been repeatedly destroyed by fire and war, and most of the existing structures date from the seventeenth century. Surrounded by maple trees, Jingo-ji is located at the top of a long flight of stone steps leading down to the Kiyotaki River. As a symbolic way to dispose of bad karma, visitors may buy small clay plates to throw from the cliff edge to the river below.

Above left A detail of the eaves of the Bishamondo. This building was used as the temple's *kondo* (main hall) until a new *kondo* was built in 1935.

Above right Sanmon (Mountain Gate).

Left The Daishido (Kobo Daishi hall) was the only building from the original temple to have survived the Onin War (1467–77), although the date of this reconstruction is unknown.

merchant townhouses

Machiya are the traditional wooden townhouses that until recently made up the majority of Kyoto's urban fabric. Generally *sukiya*-style buildings, they lined the edges of the streets in tightly packed rows, in many cases sharing party walls. Historically, land tax in Kyoto was charged based on street frontage rather than site area, encouraging the citizens to make thin, deep houses. The resulting site proportions gave them the colloquial name *unagi no nedoko* ("eel nest"). While those laws have long since been revoked, the lot divisions they caused still remain. Bringing light and air into the deeper areas of a house was achieved through the *nakaniwa* (inner garden) or *tsuboniwa* (tiny courtyard garden). These exterior spaces are located within the main volume, or between the house and secondary structures such as a *kura* (storehouse) at the rear of the site. Typically inhabited by a merchant or artisan, a machiya would have a front room used as a shop or place of business, with the pattern of *koshi* (wooden lattices) covering the street windows identifying the particular trade. From the front gate, visitors would enter a small courtyard, then step up to the tatami mats of the front room. Alternatively, family members could directly enter the kitchen, which was contained in a double-height space with a tamped earth floor, set at the same level as outside and stretching the full length of the house.

Following the Meiji Restoration of 1868, Japan embarked on an official campaign of modernization and Westernization under the rubric *wakon yosai* ("Japanese spirit, Western knowledge"). Prompted in part by the high incidence of tuberculosis, the government denigrated traditional houses as dark and unhygienic, and promoted the adoption of Western living patterns and architectural styles. In the decades following the Second World War, machiya were widely considered to be uncomfortable, primitive relics of a feudal, impoverished past. Vast numbers of them have been demolished and replaced with Western-style houses. In recent years, with a belated awareness of what has been lost, the surviving machiya are being preserved, renovated, and converted into shops, restaurants, art galleries, hotels, and occasionally even residences.

Kinpyo 金瓢

LOCATION **HIGASHIYAMA-KU**

ESTABLISHED IN **2007**

OWNER **AKIYAMA TAHEI**

Located on the northern edge of the Gion district, Kinpyo is the former home of Akiyama Tomiko (1924–97), a noted writer whose favored topics were the culture and aesthetics of Kyoto. She published books on traditional *banzai* food, the lifestyle engendered by Kyoto's *shiki* (four seasons), *kyo onna* (the women of Kyoto), tofu, and the making of saké. Her family has been producing saké for ten generations under the brand name Kinpyo, meaning "golden gourd." Symbolizing good fortune, the gourd motif can be found on all Kinpyo's bottle labels and in various places throughout this house. When Akiyama passed on, her son chose not to live in the house, but did not want to see it destroyed; it is, after all, an exquisite example of the many things that his mother loved about her home city. In 2007, assisted by architect Minami Shigeru, he converted this 200-year-old machiya into an exclusive ryokan with only two guestrooms.

Around the same time as the renovation work began, an old Kinpyo *sakegura* (saké warehouse) was being pulled down, and many of the demolition materials from it have been used in the renovation. Not only was wood from the *sakegura* used for the floorboards, the stair, and some of the pillars (the existing pillars are square in section, the *sakegura* ones are round), it was also used for making items of furniture. The bench in the ground level lobby, the *agarikamachi* step up from the *doma* (tamped earth floor) to the tatami level, and the beautiful table in the larger guestroom were all created from salvaged beams.

The old wooden chairs in the larger of the two guestrooms have been renovated using a technique called *ikkanbari*, in which the frames were covered with fabric to which multiple layers of lacquer were then applied. The entire process took one year—longer than the renovation of the building itself.

Previous spread The façade of the Kinmata ryokan.

Above Looking into the *genkan* (lobby) from the street, through the wooden slat entrance door.

Opposite above The generous double-height *genkan*. With a concrete mortar floor on which shoes are worn, this type of room is known as a *doma*. Implements for making Kinpyo saké are on display.

Opposite below left The street façade of Kinpyo. The narrow slits on the upper level are known as *mushikomado* (insect cage windows).

Opposite below right A typical street façade in the neighborhood around Kinpyo.

Above The *genkan* area is decorated with various items salvaged from one of the Kinpyo saké warehouses, such as the items of furniture against the far wall.

Left Kinpyo brand saké bottles.

Right The saké bar, where the full range of Kinpyo saké may be tasted.

Right Subtle lighting enhances the texture of the plaster walls.

Far right The *genkan* area contains a *robata* (charcoal grill), on which food is prepared for customers seated on either side. The far bench is made from heavy roof beams salvaged from a Kinpyo saké warehouse.

Bottom right Looking down into the *genkan* from the upper level of the house.

Below Traditional wooden buckets.

Bottom The traditional-style bath is made of *hinoki* (Japanese cypress), giving a distinctive scent to the room as well as the hot water.

Right The modern washroom has been sensitively designed to harmonize with the traditional architecture.

Above In the larger of the two guestrooms, which is able to comfortably hold five people, the floor is half wooden boards and half tatami mats. The latter are Okinawan style, square with no border strips.

Right A *maiko* (apprentice geisha) passes on the street outside Kinpyo, a common sight in Kyoto's Gion district.

Kinmata 近又

LOCATION **NAKAGYO-KU**

ESTABLISHED IN **1898**

OWNER **UKAI HARUJI**

Above A stone lantern sits adjacent to the discreet front entrance.

Below The softly lit central corridor is lined with sliding wooden doors, and has a view of the *tsuboniwa* enclosed garden.

Opposite The *genkan* (entrance hall). Visitors remove their shoes here, and then step onto the tatami mats of the front room, where seasonal decorations are on display.

Set right in Kyoto's commercial heart, Gokomachi-dori is now a thriving covered shopping arcade but was originally used as a ceremonial route for the Emperor. It leads directly from the Imperial Palace to the Fushimi district in the south of the city, and was created by Toyotomi Hideyoshi (1537–98) during his sixteenth-century replanning of Kyoto. The delicate, unobtrusive façade of Kinmata ryokan faces onto Gokomachi-dori, less than a minute's walk from Shijo-dori, a modern shopping boulevard to the south, and Nishiki-koji, the city's main traditional food market to the north.

Originally established in 1801 elsewhere in the same neighborhood, Kinmata moved to its current location in 1898. The building is a *sukiya*-style machiya, built as a private home as well as to provide food and temporary accommodation for the itinerant medicine traders with whom the owners did business. Every month the same clients and customers would visit and stay, but in recent decades this became increasingly difficult to sustain. The advent of the *shinkansen* high-speed train made overnight stays less common, and traveling salesmen began to prefer modern business hotels, partly due to their discomfort with the lack of privacy and security in a traditional inn, not to mention the shared bath. In the mid-1980s the despondent owners considered closing down the ryokan, retaining only the restaurant for dedicated connoisseurs. Yet, looking around the immediate neighborhood and seeing the tragic loss of so much of the traditional architecture, owner Ukai Haruji realized that he had a larger cultural responsibility and a historical legacy to preserve. He invested a great deal of time and money in restoration work that includes discreetly installed air-conditioning and modern plumbing. Today, Kinmata's seven rooms, most of them with a view of the perfectly maintained courtyard garden, are almost always occupied, and even people who do not need a place to stay will visit to savor the quality of the multicourse *kaiseki* food.

Above One of the eleven *kyakuma* (guestrooms). Tea or meals are served here, and futons laid out in the evening. The *tokonoma* alcove on the right contains a *kakejiku* hanging scroll, changed in accordance with the seasons.

Below left Each *kyakuma* has a unique layout and design. The *fusuma* panels here are decorated with images of bamboo. The *tokonoma* alcove is visible in the deepest part of the room.

Below right A sample of the justly famous *kaiseki ryori* cuisine served at Kinmata, attracting guests who come specially for the food.

Left The exquisitely composed and perfectly maintained *tsuboniwa* enclosed garden is visible from most of the rooms.

Below A detail of a decorative image on a *fusuma* panel.

Bottom A small *enkei koshimado* (circular lattice window).

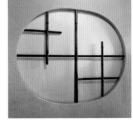

111

Inakatei 田舎亭

LOCATION **HIGASHIYAMA-KU**

BUILT IN **c.1890**

OWNER **OKUMURA IKUKO**

Above The discreet street entrance of Inakatei is located along the narrow Ishibei-koji (Stone Wall Lane), sometimes known as Omekake-dori (Street of the Concubines).

Opposite above The single guestroom on the ground floor looks out to a narrow garden that was once an artificial pond, with a stone lantern silhouetted amid the greenery.

Opposite below left A view from the upper level down to treetops and tiled roofs.

Opposite below right Pigeons gather on Nene Street, in the vicinity of Ishibei-koji.

Perhaps the most charming of Kyoto's designated historical preservation districts, Ishibei-koji (Stone Wall Lane) is a winding narrow street set in the foothills of the Higashiyama mountains and lined with traditional architecture. The name comes from its stone paving (some of which was taken from the old tramway system in Kyoto, discontinued in 1978), and from the tall stone foundation walls of the buildings either side, necessitated by the relatively steep slopes. With no cars and few pedestrians, illuminated in the evenings only by the discreet warm glow of the entrances to the *ryotei* and ryokan—simultaneously inviting and excluding—Ishibei-koji allows one to feel immersed in the atmosphere of old Kyoto. To be sure, it is all somewhat contrived, a new development that dates from no earlier than the Taisho Period (1912–26), but even so this has long been the real heart of Gion's pleasure quarters: Ishibei-koji was once known as Omekake-dori (Street of the Concubines), as many of the buildings were once luxurious homes for the mistresses of Kyoto's elite.

Partway along Ishibei-koji is the *sukiya-style* Inakatei, a former *ryotei* with a somewhat mysterious history, and now a six-room ryokan: one at ground level, four upstairs, and a tiny *chashitsu* in the garden that is used as accommodation. The current owners wished to preserve it all intact, so there are few modern conveniences. Located outside the main building, toilets are shared and the baths are communal. The garden alongside the *chashitsu* and the private garden adjoining the ground level guestroom are naturalistic compositions of moss and stones but were once ponds, which would have given the surreal impression of floating architecture. Though Inakatei no longer provides evening meals, *maiko* and *geiko* entertainment is available on request. This has always been the case: the small toilet pavilion in the front garden was once a waiting room for the retainers of the aristocrats enjoying themselves within.

Left The *engawa* (veranda) of the ground floor guest-room. This type of veranda, in which the boards run perpendicular to the building wall with the crosscut ends of the wood exposed, is known as a *kirime-en*.

Below A stone bowl set in the garden, which collects rainwater that is then used for watering plants.

Above A small ceramic *chabin* (teapot) set as a decorative element at the *genkan* (entrance hall).

Above right Ishibei-koji is lined with fences and walls, elegant compositions of wood, clay, and plaster that ensure the privacy of the various establishments and their clientele. Relatively high stone foundation walls give the lane its name.

Center right A wooden lattice window, with sliding panels made of translucent glass.

Below right The vertical wooden slats of the entrance door to the *genkan*, with a small sign on the left that reads "Inakatei" (Countryside Restaurant).

Iori Minoya-cho 庵 美濃屋町

LOCATION **PONTO-CHO**

BUILT IN c.1930

OWNER **IORI**

Above Despite its small size, the *sazanka* (Japanese camellia) tree beside the *tsukubai* (water basin) is more than a hundred years old.

Opposite above The ground level living room has undergone extensive renovations, although the decorative *ranma* lintels are original. The wood of the house itself is mainly *kitayama sugi*, a highly regarded type of Japanese cedar grown in the mountains north of Kyoto.

Opposite below left Looking north along the Kamo River in the vicinity of the house.

Opposite below right The *roji* (alleyway) alongside the house, where a rickshaw was parked in times past. The wooden gate of the *roji* has been remodeled as shoe shelves in the entry hall.

Iori is a company established in 2004 by writer and Japan expert Alex Kerr together with several like-minded colleagues. The primary ambition of Iori is to renovate and rent high-quality examples of old machiya, thereby preserving a part of Kyoto's architectural heritage and providing tourists with the experience of life in a traditional Japanese home. The renovations are not necessarily authentic, but are always sensitive to the spatial character of the old houses while updating their plumbing and other conveniences to provide a more comfortable environment. Each house contains an array of extraordinary artworks and artifacts— sculptures, scrolls, screens, calligraphy—much of it from Kerr's private collection, with no qualms about introducing modern design elements or ancient art works from other cultures.

Minoya-cho is the largest of the riverfront properties maintained by Iori, and was once the residence and clinic of a local doctor. Iori now rents out the section of the house facing the water, while the section facing the street is still used by the doctor as a consultation room. The two parts of the house are separated by an elegant courtyard garden with a sheltered *engawa* (veranda) running along the side. The garden contains a *tsukubai* (water basin) that is actually a repurposed *ishiusu*—a large stone bowl used for pounding steamed rice into *mochi* rice cakes. The adjacent tree is an ancient *sazanka* (Japanese camellia), and the garden also contains a crape myrtle, known in Japanese as a *sarusuberi*. The name literally means "monkey slide," and refers to the smooth, barkless trunks up which even a monkey will have trouble climbing; such branches are often used to make *tokobashira* decorative posts. The rear section of the house is accessed by a narrow *roji* (alley) that was in times past used as a parking spot for a rickshaw. An extremely fine example of *sukiya* carpentry, this is a generous three-level house: the lower two levels are brightly lit with full-width glass doors looking out to the river, and the topmost level is a subdued, intimate attic space.

Left A view from the ground floor living room toward the inner garden, with the doctor's consultation room visible beyond.

Above A view of the garden from the *engawa*. The tree in the foreground is a crape myrtle, known in Japan as a *sarusuberi* (monkey slide).

Below The intimate attic space on the third floor. During the renovation, glass tiles were used to create a skylight, and small glass windows were inserted on the east and north sides.

Far left An unusual triangular shelf design in the ground floor *tokonoma* alcove.

Left The *washitsu* (Japanese-style room) on the second floor facing toward the river on the east.

Left below The door pulls on the *fusuma* panels are set lower than normal, probably intended for people to politely kneel when opening and closing them.

Right Futons laid out in the streetside *washitsu* on the second floor.

Below The ground floor living room opens out toward the river.

Iori Sujiya-cho 庵 筋屋町

LOCATION **NAKAGYO-KU**

BUILT IN **c.1870**

OWNER **IORI**

Above The entry area remains in its original condition, with an absolute minimum of renovation work and no signage. To the right, a *noren* curtain flutters in the wind, indicating the route to the Origin Arts Practice Hall at the rear of the house.

Below Looking at the rear of Sujiya-cho from the courtyard in front of the Origin Arts Practice Hall.

Opposite The *itama* (room with a wooden floor), off the entry hall on the second floor, contains a *byobu* (folding screen) covered with idiosyncratic calligraphy.

One of the largest of the renovated machiya maintained by Iori, Sujiya-cho accommodates up to ten people. The house has been largely preserved in its as-found state, thus displaying the many idiosyncratic alterations and elaborations that have been made over time. As with all of the Iori properties, very little official documentation exists about the history of Sujiya-cho. The house was initially assumed to be about a hundred years old, but one day Iori received a visit from a woman in her eighties who announced that the house had once belonged to her grandfather, and provided an anecdotal history. The age of Sujiya-cho was revised to somewhere between 130 and 140 years old; it could be no older than that, as the entire neighborhood was destroyed during the Great Genji Fire of 1864. The original owner was a ship designer (and a published author on the topic), and the *washitsu* (Japanese-style room) on the ground level was his private room. The ceramic pillow on which he slept is now displayed on a shelf in the *tokonoma* alcove, next to the *butsudan* (Buddhist altar). The front room, used for business dealings, contains a *kamidana* (household Shinto shrine) to encourage prosperity. The house was later owned by a lumber dealer, and following that a soybean trader. A luxurious home, Sujiya-cho has two staircases, one for the family and the other for servants. The servant quarters were on the attic level, and are now used as a sleeping nook for guests.

Beyond simple accommodation, Iori also coordinates or hosts demonstrations of traditional art forms. Sujiya-cho can be used to hold large tea ceremonies, and to the rear of the house is the Origin Arts Practice Hall, a converted storehouse used for tea ceremony lessons while seated at tables (to aid the elderly and infirm), *no* theater demonstrations, and so on. Former US First Lady Laura Bush once spent an afternoon learning calligraphy here while her husband conferred with Prime Minister Jun'ichiro Koizumi elsewhere in Kyoto.

123

Far left All the Iori houses are decorated with an eclectic mix of antiques and art works.

Middle left The ground floor *washitsu* provides a view to the garden through vertically sliding *yukimishoji* (snow-viewing shoji).

Left A row of futons laid out on the second floor.

Left below Accessed directly from Tomino-koji Street, the tiled floor front room was formerly used for business meetings.

Below The *tokonoma* alcove in the *washitsu* on the second floor.

Left Looking down to the kitchen, with its wooden countertop, and the dining area beyond.

Below One of the many eclectic and amusing artifacts to be found in the house.

Far left Looking through to the main living area, with the courtyard garden visible beyond.

Left A stone bathtub, unique to Sujiya-cho among the ten machiya maintained by Iori.

Below The *tsukubai* (stone washbasin) in the garden is used for preparations during the tea ceremony lessons that take place at the Sujiya-cho house.

Iori Zaimoku-cho 庵 材木町

LOCATION **NAKAGYO-KU**

BUILT IN **c.1900**

OWNER **IORI**

Above The remodeled entrance incorporates a wooden door from a *kura* (traditional storehouse) flanked by two stone sculptures of *komainu*, the guardian lion-dogs found at Shinto shrines.

Below A view of the small Takase River, which flows alongside the street on which the house sits.

Opposite Looking out toward the Kamo River from the *washitsu* (Japanese-style room) on the ground floor.

Kyoto's traditional geisha culture now comprises five distinct districts, known as *hanamachi* ("flower towns"): Kamishichi-ken, Miyagawa-cho, Gion-kobu, Gion-higashi, and Ponto-cho (a sixth, Shimabara, is now defunct). The smallest of these is Ponto-cho, little more than a narrow, cobblestoned pedestrian street that runs north-south between Sanjo-dori and Shijo-dori, two of Kyoto's main commercial avenues. Adjacent to the Kamo River, Ponto-cho is now a historical preservation district, though it is still home to a thriving nightlife. The street is lined with expensive bars and restaurants, and each summer the riverside establishments construct large dining terraces that project out over the river. Walking down Ponto-cho between dusk and dawn, you will often encounter *geiko* (the Kyoto term for geisha) and *maiko* (apprentice geisha) moving between their mysterious appointments, wooden *geta* footwear clattering on the cobblestones.

Not far south of Ponto-cho, and also facing onto the Kamo River, Iori Zaimoku-cho is a small riverfront machiya that was once the private home of a Ponto-cho *geiko* and is now one of the properties maintained by the Iori company. At some point in the house's history, the front section was demolished and converted into a car parking area, leaving only the compact *nagaya* (row house) section to the rear. Having been partially renovated by the Kyoto design-and-build office Noguchi Group, the interior is a subtle mixture of cool modernism and traditional elements. A pivoting glass door allows a sightline right through the house, from the entry hall to the river and mountains in the far distance. The simple balcony of weather-beaten planks is an ideal place to watch the changing of the seasons—cherry blossom trees lining the river in spring, red foliage on the Higashiyama mountain range in autumn, gulls and egrets playing in the river during winter (the best season for bird watching). Long-term residents of the neighborhood recall that this is where the *geiko* would practice her shamisen.

128

Above left Dating from the Edo Period (1603–1868), the *byobu* (folding screen) affixed to the wall shows a scene from the Gion Matsuri, one of Kyoto's most important annual festivals.

Left The view from the house looking north along the Kamo River, with the Kitayama mountains visible in the distance.

Left Illuminated by discreet hidden lighting, futons are laid out in the *washitsu* on the second floor.

Below left Beyond the *washitsu* on the second floor is a small sitting area with a wooden floor.

Above A flock of black-headed gulls settled alongside the river. Visitors from the Asian continent, these birds are only found here in winter.

Below A balcony projects toward the river from the ground floor *washitsu*, with the Higashiyama mountains visible above the buildings on the other side.

Iori Sanbo Nishinotoin-cho

庵 三坊西洞院町

LOCATION **NAKAGYO-KU**

BUILT IN **1885**

OWNER **IORI**

Above The garden in front of the *washitsu* (Japanese-style room) on the lower level, with *geta* footwear arrayed in front of the *engawa*.

Built in 1885, Sanbo Nishinotoin-cho was originally a famous embroidery shop, and examples of the work produced here were exhibited at a World's Fair in Paris during the late nineteenth century. As a result of the national austerity imposed by the Second World War, pursuits such as embroidery were seen as an unconscionable extravagance and the shop was closed down. After the war, the house became an atelier for the painter Kobayashi Uko (1895–1976), a graduate of the Kyoto City Specialist School of Painting, now known as the Kyoto City University of Arts. A cosmopolitan figure who lived in France during 1920–21, Uko was also a close friend of the writers Tanizaki Jun'ichiro (1886–1965) and Akutagawa Ryunosuke (1892–1927); the former was a Nobel Prize-winning novelist and the latter was widely known as the "father of the Japanese short story." For a period the house became something of a cultural salon, and later it was converted into a kimono shop. While a small kimono showroom still survives, since 2007 the section of the house fronting the street has been occupied by the Motoan Tea House. Entirely unrelated to the geisha *ochaya* or the tea ceremony *chashitsu*, this is a *sabo*, a shop selling *matcha* (green tea) and *wagashi* (Japanese sweets). Motoan is a branch of the venerable Marukyu-Koyamaen Company, which has been cultivating and preparing tea plants in the Uji area outside Kyoto for many centuries.

Beyond the small courtyard garden visible from inside Motoan, the rear part of the house is maintained by the Iori company as a rental property. There is a tea ceremony room on the first floor, facing onto a private garden to the rear. Upstairs is a high-ceilinged space with wooden floorboards and two original rocking chairs, now reupholstered. This was where Uko painted, and large picture windows still flood the space with natural light.

Left The *sukiya*-style entry was added during the remodeling, and incorporates the *nijiriguchi* (crawl-in entrance) of the original *chashitsu*. To the left is a *shiorido* bamboo gate leading to the garden.

Above The living room on the upper level. The calligraphy on the *byobu* (folding screen) attached to the wall is the work of Sawada Minoru, one of Iori's guest instructors in Japanese culture, who did the middle section, and Iori founder Alex Kerr, who did the outer two characters. The table is a recycled door from a *kura* (storehouse).

Top left The calligraphy in the *tokonoma* is the work of an anonymous *daimyo* (feudal lord). Reading right to left, it says *afureru-ai* ("overflowing with love").

Top right Looking from the entry hall to the *washitsu* on the lower level. The *chashitsu* lies beyond the *fusuma* panels on the right.

Center left The *washitsu* on the upper level. The *byobu* is the work of Kobayashi Uko, and comprises twelve separate paintings, mostly of plants and animals. There is a similar *byobu* in the *washitsu* on the lower level.

Center right The stair leading from the entry hall to the upper level.

Opposite below The bathtub is made of *hinoki* (Japanese cypress). Visible outside is a tiny, ancient shrine to the sea goddess Benten.

Above The *washitsu* on the lower level, with a view of the garden beyond.

Right A stone water basin in the garden.

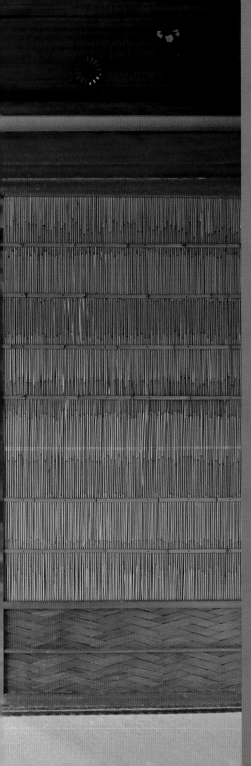

traditional inns

Generally thought of as a traditional Japanese inn, the ryokan has no clear or precise definition. From tiny establishments with only a couple of rooms to vast resort complexes, from authentic traditional buildings to modern concrete structures, from inexpensive, casual accommodation to a once-in-a-lifetime aesthetic experience, the ryokan is more than a building type. It is a form of behavior, a system of etiquette, a state of mind. Guests will generally wash in a communal bath, change into *yukata* (a light cotton robe), and be served *kaiseki ryori* (a varied series of small traditional dishes) in their rooms. With the meal cleared away, futons will be laid out on the tatami mat floor, and all the members of the group will sleep in the same room. Some ryokan provide geisha entertainment, others emphasize the variety of bathing options, both indoor and outdoor. While staying at a ryokan may give a sense of traditional daily life in Japan, an authentic experience of the lifestyle of the aristocracy is only to be found at the most exclusive and expensive places.

There are two main types of ryokan: inns for travelers, and tourist resorts set among natural hot springs. The former type arose during the Edo Period (1603–1868) along the nation's main transportation routes, notably the Tokaido road linking Kyoto and Edo. Provincial lords were required to periodically visit Edo, so they and their large retinues needed places to stay along the way. The officially designated rest stops for the nobles were grand *shoin*-style buildings called *honjin*. The lower ranking members of their parties would stay in *hatagoya*, smaller establishments that also catered to merchants, pilgrims, and sightseers. In the late Edo Period, *honjin* also became available to commoners when not being used by nobles. The romance of travel along these roads was popularized by their depictions in various sets of woodblock prints, most famously *Tokaido Gojusan Tsuginouchi* (The Fifty-three Stations of the Tokaido), rendered in more than thirty different versions by the renowned artist Utagawa Hiroshige (1797–1858). The many merchants making regular visits to Kyoto also required places for food and accommodation in the city itself, and these are the origin of most of the traditional ryokan surviving today.

Hiiragiya 柊家

LOCATION **NAKAGYO-KU**

BUILT IN **1818 / ANNEX IN 2006**

ORIGINAL OWNER **NISHIMURA SHOZABURO**

Previous spread A guestroom in Yoshida Sanso.

Above The view from the sheltered entry courtyard into the lobby.

Below Female members of staff are known by the historical term *jochu-san* (maidservant).

Opposite above The new *hiroma* (banquet hall) provides an uninterrupted view of the garden through its glass walls—modern construction techniques used to achieve the traditional ambiguous boundary between inside and outside.

Opposite below left In the sheltered area leading from the street to the *genkan* (entry hall), the stone paving is kept constantly wet to create a cool, fresh atmosphere and as a sign of welcome for the guests.

Opposite below right A distinctive window design in which the lower triangular element is intended to echo the roof forms of the main building, visible outside.

Located far from the seacoast in every direction, Kyoto's traditional cuisine was necessarily focused on pickled and preserved food. Nevertheless, there was always a demand for the freshest possible fish, and Hiiragiya was established in 1818 as a trading house specializing in seafood brought in along the Sabakaido (Mackerel Road) from the Japan Sea coast. Located within easy reach of the traditional city markets at Nishiki-koji and Sanjo-ohashi, Hiiragiya was used as casual accommodation by the fish traders, and became officially registered as a ryokan in 1861. Hiiragiya has been run by the same family for six generations. A placard with the motto *kuru mono, kaeru gotoshi* ("visitors feel that they have come home") was placed in the lobby by the third-generation owner during the Meiji Period (1868–1912). The fourth-generation owner created unique handmade light fittings for every room—wooden boxes with a holly leaf motif (*hiiragi* is a native Japanese tree that resembles holly). Indeed, each room is unique in its design, and—as with all of Kyoto's most exclusive ryokans—guests are barely aware of each other's presence.

The original building has twenty-one rooms, and an annex designed by architect Michida Jun (1968–) was completed in 2005. The annex contains seven new rooms in a modernized *sukiya* style, together with a large *hiroma* (banquet hall). The *hiroma* has no pillars—its structure is suspended from the fence that encloses the site, allowing an uninterrupted view of the garden through glass walls. A discrete, serene oasis, Hiiragiya is located in the commercial heart of Kyoto, where wood-framed buildings have become illegal. Maintaining an existing wood building is still acceptable, but major renovations will entail switching to a steel or concrete structure. The owners of Hiiragiya are doing their best to preserve this extraordinary piece of Kyoto's historical legacy as long as they possibly can.

Opposite An *ogi-chirashi* (scattered folding fan) design has been applied to the *fusuma* panels in this guestroom, which is contained in the main building.

Left A corner alcove in one of the guestrooms in the main building.

Below Images of *hana-guruma* (flower carts) decorate the *fusuma* panels in this guestroom, located in the main building.

Left A view of the superb Japanese garden located to the rear of the main building.

Above A gridded shoji panel framing a view of a tiny *tsuboniwa* (enclosed garden).

Right Soft light enters through the frosted glass of this corner window in the new annex.

Right One of the rooms in the new annex has been equipped with western-style beds and other amenities. The wallpaper is *furobaki* style, comprising overlapping sheets of handmade *washi* paper.

Far right A bathtub made of *koyamaki* wood, a conifer native to Japan.

Left A room in the new annex, designed in a simplified, abstracted version of the *sukiya* style. The ceiling panels are made of *yoshino sugi*, a special grade of Japanese cedar.

Gion Hatanaka 祇園 畑中

LOCATION **HIGASHIYAMA-KU**

BUILT IN **1962 / ANNEX IN 1996**

ORIGINAL OWNER **HATANAKA TOSHIO**

Opposite above left The entrance gate of Gion Hatanaka, leading from the street to the lobby.

Opposite above right An inner courtyard garden that contains a large *toro* (stone lantern).

Opposite below The lobby has an enormous picture window looking onto another courtyard garden.

Below A *maiko* performer displaying the back of the spectacular *obi* (sash) that binds her kimono.

The role of the geisha—a combination of professional hostess, traditional entertainer, and cultivated courtesan—has a long and complex lineage, but the word itself (literally translated as "art person") appeared in the eighteenth century and was originally applied to male performers. The males were soon supplanted in popularity by the female version, although the stereotypical image of a slim, serene girl with white face makeup, an ornate kimono, and an elaborate hairstyle is, in fact, a *maiko*, a trainee geisha. Kyoto's Gion district remains one of Japan's few remaining centers of geisha (known locally as *geiko*) culture, yet their numbers are a tiny fraction of what they were during the Edo Period (1603–1868). Seeing them is not easy, aside from at occasional public events, and almost impossible in their natural habitat of an *ochaya* (a word usually and confusingly translated into English as "tea house"; the *ochaya* is a commercial establishment entirely unrelated to the *chashitsu* used for the tea ceremony). Newcomers need an introduction from a regular customer to visit *ochaya*, which are expensive and exclusive places, a practice known as *ichigensan okotowari* (first-timers refused).

The characteristic *maiko* and *geiko* traditions of Kyoto are said to have originated with a pair of *ochaya* that once flanked the south gate of Yasaka Shrine—the Nakamuraya and Fujiya, known collectively as Nikenchaya. Their owners decided to improve business by having the waitresses learn to sing and dance, and the rest is history. Nikenchaya may no longer be in business, but a very short distance away is the Gion Hatanaka ryokan, one of the few places in Kyoto where anyone may see authentic *maiko* in a setting similar to a real *ochaya*. Entered via a flight of stone steps to a deceptively small and discreet entrance, Gion Hatanaka is a beautifully designed and maintained *sukiya*-style inn comprising nine original rooms and twelve rooms built in a recent renovation. Guests receive *kaiseki* food and *maiko* entertainment, which, in keeping with tradition, begins as elegant *maiko* dances accompanied by a *geiko* playing a shamisen and ends as raucous drinking games with audience participation.

Below left The guest-rooms are floored partly in tatami mats and partly in wooden boards, with a view out to a *tsuboniwa* (enclosed garden).

Below right The audience watches the *maiko* performance over dinner in the 56-mat banquet room.

Above A garden viewed through a wooden lattice.

Right A decorative lantern.

Above A *maiko* dance accompanied by shamisen music, against the backdrop of a gold leaf-clad *byobu* (folding screen).

Right The final course of the *kaiseki* meal.

Rangetsu 嵐月

LOCATION **UKYO-KU**

BUILT IN **2005**

ORIGINAL OWNER **SATO EIKO**

Above Though the old rear garden has been preserved from the previous ryokan, this front garden was laid out during the construction of Rangetsu.

Opposite above Looking down on the double-height lobby—a worthy attempt to meld modern hotel design standards with a *sukiya*-style sensibility.

Out on the western periphery of Kyoto, the Arashiyama district was a popular locale for country villas belonging to the nobility of the Heian Period (794–1185). Blessed with mountains, forests, rivers, bamboo thickets, cherry blossom groves, and monkey colonies, the area still has an exotic beauty that inevitably attracts huge numbers of tourists. The main business is *ryotei ryokan*, luxurious traditional inns providing superb traditional food. The most prestigious face directly onto the Oi River, a short stretch of shallow water that connects the Katsura River in the east to the Hozu River in the west. The river's name change occurs at the exact spot the water is straddled by the Togetsukyo (Moon Crossing Bridge), one of Arashiyama's best-known historical landmarks.

Located a short distance from Togetsukyo is Rangetsu (Storm Moon), a riverfront ryokan that was completed in 2005, replacing another ryokan on the same site. The rear garden survives from the previous building, but Rangetsu is otherwise entirely new, designed and built by a Nara-based carpentry company called Asanuma-gumi. The design is a modernized version of *sukiya*-style architecture at a much larger scale— the idiosyncrasy is maintained, though unavoidably some of the intimacy is lost. Rangetsu is focused on the experience of bathing. The communal baths use warm water drawn from an underground spring and further heated artificially (Rangetsu does not qualify as an *onsen*, which requires a natural water temperature of at least 25 degrees centigrade). The fifteen rooms are all subtly different in size, design, and outlook. With a large courtyard garden in the middle, the front wing faces the river and the rear wing looks out to the forested Mount Atago. Each of the three deluxe rooms has a private garden containing a *rotenburo* (outdoor bath) in the form of a large ceramic tub, and a unique design theme for its colors and decorative elements: red maple leaves, pink cherry blossoms, and blue water. A small *chashitsu* next to the entrance hall is used to hold *chado* lessons for interested guests.

Far left The lobby contains moon and bamboo motifs, also found elsewhere in the building.

Left Looking out from the main corridor to the front garden.

Above left A ceramic *rotenburo* (open-air bath) sits in the private garden that adjoins each of the three deluxe rooms.

Above right Small *akari-torishoji*, sliding panels intended to bring in daylight.

Left One of the three private gardens facing out toward the Oi River.

Near right Modern shoji screens with a distinctive *ranma* (open lintel) above.

Center right A lustrous black lacquer table accented with gold leaf in one of the deluxe guestrooms.

Far right An unusual curving *tokonoma* design, containing a *kakejiku* (hanging scroll).

Left A modern interpretation of traditional shoji screen designs.

Below A detail of the drainage channel in the front garden. Cylindrical chunks of charcoal are contained between ceramic tiles embedded sideways in the gravel.

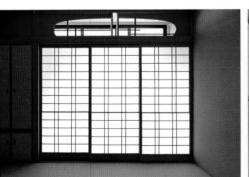

Jijuden 仁寿殿ゲストハウス京都

LOCATION **KITA-KU**

ESTABLISHED IN **2008**

OWNER **UESHIMA YOKO**

Above This is a modernized version of the *tsuboniwa* (enclosed courtyard garden) in the lobby of the new wing, which contains all the guestrooms.

Opposite A view from the new wing to the renovated old house. Between the two is a spacious courtyard and garden containing objects and materials salvaged during the renovation.

Like every culture, Japan has evolved a characteristic palette of colors, arising out of the interplay between local preferences and available materials. Some hues originated with dyes derived from plants and animals and have been in use for over a millennium whereas others are synthetic chemical compounds developed in modern times, yet they are predominantly delicate, subdued colors arising from, and well suited to, the Japanese climate. The local spectrum comprises extraordinarily subtle distinctions, each color given its own evocative name. Accurate sample swatches have been rigorously maintained over the centuries, compiled in thick color guidebooks. At Jijuden, a modern ryokan located on the west side of Kyoto—halfway between the Golden Pavilion of Kinkaku-ji and the stone garden of Ryoan-ji— the seven guestrooms do not have numbers but rather colors. Each is named after a traditional hue that also delicately infuses its interior design palette: *choji* (a nutmeg brown), *hanada* (a blue often used in Imperial robes), *suo* (a red-brown common in traditional kimono fabrics), *byakuroku* (a natural green), *shikon* (a dull purple), *kihada* (a yellow also favored by the Imperial family), and *roko* (a black-brown named after a famous kabuki actor, it being his favorite color).

Prior to opening Jijuden, the owners were involved in making and selling kimonos, hence their interest in the subtleties of balancing hues. They converted their own *sukiya*-style home into a guesthouse intended to combine the best aspects of the Japanese ryokan and the English bed-and-breakfast. The old house now contains a café, an informal library of books and CDs, and a *chashitsu* still used for holding tea ceremonies. The guest wing is entirely new, an elegant example of East-meets-West minimalism designed with sensitive attention to detail by Kyoto architect Sugiki Genzo (1951–). Between the two is a new courtyard garden utilizing objects and materials salvaged during the renovation.

Left The façade of the new wing is partly clad in closely spaced vertical wooden slats, evoking and updating a traditional motif.

Left The old house now contains a library and lounge space for guests, full of books on Kyoto and Japanese culture.

Below The *chashitsu* in the old *sukiya*-style house has been preserved and renovated, and is available for guests interested in experiencing a traditional tea ceremony.

Far left A traditional paper umbrella, available for transit between the two wings during bad weather.

Center left The guestrooms all contain Western-style beds, a private bathroom and a mini-kitchen. Visible through the glass is the lush Japanese-style garden.

Left A ceramic *chawan* (tea cup), accompanied by *wagashi* (Japanese sweets) and a decorative maple leaf.

Momijiya もみぢ家

LOCATION **UKYO-KU**
ESTABLISHED IN **1907**
OWNER **YAMAMOTO TOSHIKO**

Above The suspension bridge that leads across the valley to the inn.

Below The reception façade, decorated with large kanji characters that read "Momijiya."

Opposite The Kiyotaki River, located in the valley below Momijiya, against the backdrop of a mountainside covered in *kitayama sugi*, a special grade of Japanese cedar.

One of Japan's most famous modern writers, Mishima Yukio (1925–70) was a versatile if uneven artist who published a great many novels, short stories, serialized novellas, essay collections, and plays. He was shortlisted for the Nobel Prize for Literature three times. However, Mishima's increasingly fascist and nationalistic political views led to his formation of a small private army called the Tatenokai (Shield Society). Their fundamental aim was to restore and ensure the Emperor's role as the divine essence of the nation. On November 25, 1970, Mishima and four of his followers forcibly occupied a Japanese Self Defense Force office in Tokyo. From the balcony Mishima read a manifesto intended to incite a revolution, but was ridiculed and abused by the soldiers assembled below. Returning inside, he calmly committed ritual suicide, slitting open his belly and then being beheaded by a Tatenokai member. Some believe that the abortive coup attempt was really an elaborate pretext for Mishima to publicly take his own life, thus ensuring his (somewhat dubious) place in history.

Two weeks before his death, Mishima took his family on a final trip, staying at the Momijiya ryokan (also known as Takao Sanso) high in the mountains west of Kyoto. While there he gave the owners two pieces of his own calligraphy, which are now framed and on permanent display. Momijiya is located on Mount Takao, and has for decades provided food and accommodation to pilgrims on their way to Jingo-ji, a Shingon Buddhist temple established in the eighth century. The mountain is covered in forests of *kitayama sugi*, a special grade of Japanese cedar, and Momijiya is near to abundant cherry blossoms and maple trees as well as some beautiful flower gardens containing azaleas and rhododendrons. This is a place for immersing oneself in the changing of the seasons—to relax and observe the spectacular views of changing colors in the surrounding foliage, while enjoying the cuisine made from locally available ingredients.

Far left above A private *rotenburo* (open-air bath) attached to the Asagiri villa, which contains a pair of rooms each eight tatami mats in area. This is part of the more traditional Kawa-no-iori annex, separate from the main building of Momijiya.

Far left below Wooden buckets and stool used for bathing in the *rotenburo*.

Left A private *rotenburo* (open-air bath) attached to the Hototogisu room, the second of the detached villas that form part of the Kawa-no-iori annex.

Right above A view of the *tokonoma* alcove in the Asagiri villa.

Right below The serene, symmetrical interior of the Asagiri villa, partly illuminated by skylights.

Left A *jizaikagi* (adustable hook) used to hang a *nabe* (pot) for cooking over the indoor hearth.

Below Eclectic decorations in the enclosed garden of the lobby.

Right above Meals may be eaten *alfresco*, with a view of the mountainside greenery.

Right below The restaurant faces the river, and seasonal cuisine (wild mountain vegetables in spring, charcoal-grilled river trout in summer, *matsutake* mushrooms in autumn, *nabe* hotpot in winter) is served on the *kawadoko* (riverside veranda).

Yoshida Sanso 吉田山荘

LOCATION **SAKYO-KU**

BUILT IN **1932**

ORIGINAL OWNER **COUNT HIGASHIFUSHIMI KUNIHIDE**

Above Two pairs of *geta* (wooden sandals) sitting on a *kutsunugi-ishi* (shoe removing stone) in front of an *engawa* (veranda).

Located on a secluded site in the foothills of Mount Yoshida, this house was originally built as a second residence for Count Higashifushimi Kunihide (1910–), the brother-in-law of Emperor Hirohito (1901–89) and uncle of the present Emperor, Akihito (1933–). He lived here while a student at Kyoto University, located nearby. In 1943 the Count became the *monzeki* abbot of Kyoto's Shoren-in temple, and in 1948 the house was converted into a ryokan called Yoshida Sanso.

Yoshida Sanso is a sophisticated example of *shoin*-style architecture. It was built by *miya daiku* (temple carpenters) under the direction of famed artisan Nishioka Tsunekazu (1908–95), and is primarily constructed of *kiso hinoki*, Japanese cypress from the same forest that is used for the ritual reconstructions of Ise Shrine. Set at a short distance from the main building is Satsuki Cottage, a *sukiya*-style building made entirely from *kitayama sugi*, a high quality Japanese cedar predominantly used in aristocratic villas and tea houses. Decorative elements from many cultures and historical eras are scattered throughout Yoshida Sanso; one may discover everything from Chinese motifs to Hebrew script incorporated in the interior and exterior fittings. The abstract design of the stained glass window in the entry hall appears to be Art Deco in inspiration but is, in fact, taken from the pattern on the reverse side of a fourth-century bronze mirror discovered in 1884 during archaeological excavations in the Shin'yama Kofun, an enormous tomb mound located near Nara. The Imperial *kamon* (family crest)—a stylized sixteen-petal chrysanthemum—also appears throughout the building on everything from roof tiles to door handles.

The Japanese garden surrounding the house contains an array of perfectly manicured cherry blossom trees and azalea bushes, and is occasionally used as a venue for serving tea or hosting musical performances. The proprietors also commission art and craft works for sale here, and sponsor cultural events elsewhere in Japan.

Left The south façade, which looks onto the main garden and its fastidiously trimmed plants.

Below left The interior of the *genkan* (entry hall).

Below right The entry gate, with an affixed plaque that reads "Yoshida Sanso."

Far left Nakamura Kyoko and Nakamura Tomoko, the *okami* (proprietor) and *waka-okami* (her apprentice and daughter) of Yoshida Sanso.

Left The guest of honor is always seated directly in front of the *tokonoma* alcove.

Left below The rooms of this historical structure are all immaculately maintained.

Right The Western-style chairs and stained glass windows exemplify the eclecticism of Yoshida Sanso.

Below left A view of the garden from one of the second floor rooms.

Below center A *chozubachi* (stone basin) in the garden.

Below right The contrasting dishes of *kaiseki* cuisine.

Above The east façade and the projecting volume of the *genkan*. The famous circular stained glass window is visible on the left.

Above One of the many dishes served during a typical *kaiseki ryori* meal.

Above right Looking out to the garden through hanging *sudare* (reed blinds).

Right The corner of one of the guestrooms, with large windows that bring the outdoor scenery indoors.

Miyamaso 美山荘

LOCATION **SAKYO-KU**

ESTABLISHED IN **1937**

BUILT FOR **NAKAHIGASHI KICHIJI**

As authentic *sukiya* architecture becomes ever scarcer in present-day Kyoto, so do *daiku* (carpenters) with the skills to realize it. Over the last century, the city's pool of traditional artisans has become increasingly smaller, older, and underutilized. The materials and assembly methods of *sukiya* are inherently fragile, requiring frequent repairs and replacement of parts, so preserving this architectural heritage requires simultaneously maintaining its specialized techniques as living traditions. Historically, the *sukiya daiku* were divided into hereditary guilds, and the most famous of them still active in Kyoto is Nakamura Sotoji Komuten, named for its founder Nakamura Sotoji (1906–97) and now run by his son, Nakamura Yoshiaki (1946–). Sotoji is personally responsible for many prestigious structures in Japan, including the *chashitsu* at Ise Shrine and an extension to the famous Tawaraya ryokan in Kyoto. The latter was designed by the architect Yoshimura Junzo (1908–97), who also collaborated with Sotoji to build the Japanese exhibition house for the 1954 "House in the Garden" exhibition held at New York's Museum of Modern Art. This led to another famous US commission, a *chashitsu* in the grounds of Kykuit, the John D. Rockefeller Estate in Westchester, completed in 1962.

Built by Sotoji and still maintained by his company, Miyamaso (Beautiful Mountain Villa) is an exclusive *ryori* ryokan located in the mountains north of Kyoto. Originally this site contained a *tatchu* (subtemple) of nearby Bujo-ji temple, which was founded in 1154 by Emperor Toba (1103–56). In 1895 the *tatchu* was replaced by a *shukubo* (pilgrims' lodgings) for visitors to the temple. Miyamaso was established in 1937, and its main building is a reconstruction of the *shukubo* carried out by Sotoji along with the addition of various other new structures. Today Miyamaso is famous for its *tsumikusa* cuisine, which is based on the use of seasonal wild vegetables, herbs, and fish.

Above Nakahigashi Sachiko, the *waka-okami* of Miyamaso. An *okami* is the female owner or proprietor of a ryokan, and the *waka-okami* is her younger apprentice, more often than not her daughter.

Opposite above A balcony projecting from one of the guestrooms out into the forest.

Opposite below left A mountain path enlivened by the colors of fallen leaves, with the roof tiles of Miyamaso just visible through the spectacular autumn foliage.

Opposite below right The approach through the trees toward the main building.

Right The boldly illustrated *fusuma* panels in one of the guestrooms.

Below A *tokonoma* alcove, comprising a sophisticated combination of straight and naturally irregular elements.

Right The fluid, interpenetrating spaces of a guestroom.

Below near right The baths may not have access to an underground hotspring but they do use heated rainwater collected on the mountain. The river is visible outside.

Below middle right An example of Miyamaso's renowned *tsumikusa* cuisine, which is based on the use of seasonal wild vegetables, herbs, and fish.

Below far right The weathered wooden planks of an *engawa*.

private retreats

In 1895, as part of the 1100th anniversary of the founding of Heian-kyo, Kyoto hosted the Fourth National Industrial Exposition, intended to convey to the general public the various achievements of modern Japan. Held for four months in the Okazaki district, east of downtown Kyoto, the centerpiece was a five-eighths scale partial replica of the original Heian Palace, designed by architect Ito Chuta (1867–1954). At the conclusion of the Expo, the building became known as Heian Jingu shrine, in which Emperor Kammu (737–806) was then deified as Kyoto's ancestral god. The Expo itself was part of a comprehensive campaign to modernize the city. A tram system was implemented for visitors, and the following decade saw massive investments in public infrastructure: waterworks, a street-car network, hydroelectric power, paved roads. Concurrent with the Expo, the city's major temples and shrines held "treasure exhibitions," public displays of their collected antiquities and icons. The rich legacy of Kyoto's history was, if only for a brief moment, presented alongside the city's future-oriented ambitions.

Kyoto's historical traditions and modern innovations have never been seen as opposites, but rather as part of an evolving continuum. Needless to say, what are now considered venerable traditions were once radical, controversial novelties. As proud as they are of their heritage, the citizens of Kyoto have not allowed it to become stifling. The traditional craft industries continue to explore artistic and technological possibilities. New art forms are quickly adopted and developed; the city has long been a center for experimental cinema, performance, and installation art. As the cultural heart of Japan, Kyoto contains a huge number of official National Treasures and Important Cultural Properties, but more importantly, it has been home to many of those artisans designated Living National Treasures, often members of familial and guild lineages that extend as far back as the city's founding. The aesthetic formats and techniques that have accumulated over time are used as a basis for invention. Kyoto's spectacular seasonal changes, the philosophical and aesthetic sensibility of the Zen Buddhist temples, and the legacy of a millennium of creativity continue to attract people passionate about maintaining traditions as well as individuals aspiring to extend those same traditions. Between them, they keep Kyoto's culture vibrant, vital, and authentic. The former houses of many of these greater and lesser talents are now maintained as museums of their own work and life.

Shisendo 詩仙堂

LOCATION **SAKYO-KU**

BUILT IN **1641**

ORIGINAL OWNER **ISHIKAWA JOZAN**

Previous spread Daijo-kaku, the main building of Okouchi Sanso.

Above Enclosed by bamboo fences, stone steps lead through a forested slope to Shisendo.

Below The main entrance, with a distinctive Chinese-influenced window design, provides a glimpse through to the inner garden on the south side of the building.

Opposite The rooms on the south side may be entirely opened to the garden, removing any clear boundaries between inside and outside.

Of samurai lineage, Ishikawa Jozan (1583–1672) was a retainer to Tokugawa Ieyasu (1543–1616), the first of the Tokugawa shoguns. Disobedience during battle led to Ishikawa's dismissal, and at the age of thirty-three he turned to a life of scholarship in Kyoto, studying Chinese poetry and Confucian philosophy. He eventually became a famed poet and calligrapher. When his mother fell ill, he was temporarily forced into gainful employment with the Asano clan in Hiroshima, but upon her death he immediately returned to Kyoto and began construction of a small hermitage in the mountains northeast of the city, emulating the reclusive poets he so admired. He called it Oto-tsuka (Dwelling on Uneven Ground) in reference to the sloping site. Together with philosopher Hayashi Razan (1583–1657), Jozan drew up a list of what he considered to be the thirty-six greatest Chinese poets from the Han and Song Dynasties, and then commissioned the artist Kano Tan'yu (1602–74) to paint their (imagined) portraits. These have been hung in a room called Shisen-no-ma, which gives the building its popular name, Shinsendo (Hall of the Hermit Poets).

The architecture is primarily *shoin* style infused with idiosyncratic touches of *sukiya*, notably in the cupola with its circular window. Jozan labeled this the Shogetsuro, which might be translated as "tower for reciting poetry to the moon." Only the Shisen-no-ma and Shogetsuro date from Jozan's time, the rest being later additions or reconstructions. The superb gardens were designed by Jozan himself, and comprise abstracted miniatures of famous landscapes known as the "ten locales" and "twelve scenes." He is also reputed to have invented the *shishi odoshi* ("deer frightener"), a pivoting bamboo tube through which water constantly flows, causing it to periodically overbalance and loudly tap the adjacent rock. Now officially known as Jozan-ji temple, in 1966 Shisendo became a branch of Eihei-ji temple in Fukui Prefecture, one of the two main temples of Soto Zen Buddhism.

Far left The Zangetsuken tea house is located to the west of the inner garden.

Left The *zazendo* (meditation hall), known as Juppomyohokaku, is located even further west, beyond the tea house.

Above The inner garden as seen from the southernmost room. A field of raked white sand is surrounded by an array of *karikomi* (azalea bushes sculpted into spherical forms), all set against a backdrop of maple trees, their autumnal leaves a brilliant crimson.

Left Shisen-no-ma, a room containing portraits of what Ishikawa Jozan, Shisendo's creator, considered to be the thirty-six greatest Chinese poets from the Han and Song Dynasties. They were painted by the noted artist Kano Tan'yu.

Below Another view of the inner garden.

Okouchi Sanso　大河内山荘

LOCATION **UKYO-KU**

BUILT IN **1939**

ORIGINAL OWNER **OKOUCHI DENJIRO**

Above A path through the bamboo forests that cover much of the Arashiyama district.

Below A path composed of natural stones set among well-maintained moss.

Opposite Daijokaku, the main building of Okouchi Sanso, combines aspects of the *shinden*, *shoin*, and *sukiya* styles, and was built by contemporary tea house designer Usui Kaichiro based on Okouchi Denjiro's design ideas.

Stage and screen actor Okouchi Denjiro (1898–1962) may have starred in serious films made by figures such as Kurosawa Akira (1910–98), Japan's most celebrated director, but he is best remembered for the comedic character Tange Sazen, a crazed, one-armed, one-eyed *ronin* (masterless samurai). Later reprised by a number of other actors, it is a role he played often and with great dedication; his extreme shortsightedness often resulted in him being injured during the swordfight scenes.

Denjiro was also a devout Buddhist, and in 1931 he built a *jibutsudo* (private Buddha hall) in the Arashiyama district to the west of Kyoto. It is set at the foot of Mount Ogura, famous as the place where Fujiwara Teika (1162–1241), arguably the greatest of classical Japanese poets, compiled the *Ogura Hyakunin'isshu* (Ogura Anthology of One Hundred Poems by One Hundred Poets). This building became the starting point for Okouchi Sanso, a vast estate now covering 20,000 square meters of open land on the southeast face of the mountain. Using most of the large sums of money he earned playing supporting roles in stage plays, Denjiro spent the final three decades of his life developing the spectacular *kaiyushiki teien* (stroll garden), which incorporates the *shakkei* (borrowed scenery) of Mount Arashi to the east, Hozukyo Gorge to the west, and Mount Hiei in the far distance. Daijokaku, the main villa, combines aspects of the *shinden*, *shoin*, and *sukiya* styles, and was executed by contemporary tea house designer Usui Kaichiro (1898–1969) based on Denjiro's own ideas. The garden also contains a tea house called Tekisuian, and a pavilion called Gekkatei with a view of the city below. Since Denjiro's death his family has been maintaining the estate. A memorial hall in the garden now displays photos and film stills from throughout his career.

Above A spectacular view from the Gekkatei pavilion looking over the forested mountainside toward the city.

Right The entrance to the Tekisuian tea house.

Far left The Chumon (Central Gate) on the path to Daijokaku.

Left The *jibutsudo* (private Buddha hall), the humble starting point of what was to become a huge mountainside estate.

Below Stepping stones along the network of hillside paths.

Hakusasonso 橋本関雪記念館

LOCATION **SAKYO-KU**

BUILT IN **1916**

BUILT FOR **HASHIMOTO KANSETSU**

Opposite Ceramic-tiled roofs and hanging *sudare* (reed blinds) glimpsed across the pond. Originally flat land, the rolling garden landscape was designed by Kensetsu and represents years of painstaking work. It is filled with the many stone sculptures he collected during his lifetime.

Above Zonkoro, Kensetsu's studio, is a monumental three-story building that overlooks the pond.

Below Stepping stones leading through an open gate, the thatch of its roof now hidden under moss.

Born in Kobe, Hashimoto Kansetsu (1883–1945) was a writer and painter who spent most of his life in Kyoto. The son of artist Hashimoto Kaikan, from whom he absorbed a deep love of Chinese culture, Kansetsu showed an early aptitude at painting. He studied at Chikujokai, a private art school in Kyoto established by artist Takeuchi Seiho (1864–42), the leading *nihonga* (Japanese-style painting) artist of his era. Kansetsu's strong opinions on art, his criticisms of his contemporaries, his desire to revive classical traditions, and his simultaneous struggle to find a new, modern style eventually alienated him from the rest of the Kyoto art world. He made frequent trips to China, and many of his paintings were inspired by Chinese scenery or Chinese classical literature.

Hakusasonso (White Sand Villa), his former residence in Kyoto, is now a museum of his work. Having completed the main house and large studio in 1916, he spent many years developing the design of the stroll garden, focused around a *koi* (carp) pond and using Mount Daimonji and Mount Hiei as a backdrop. It is dotted with bridges, pagodas, stepping stones, sculptures, and a collection of sad-faced Buddha statues. Like a Japanese John Soane, Kansetsu collected antiquities and exotica from all over the world, and his extraordinary collection is exhibited on a rotating basis.

There are currently three restaurants on the grounds, and Kansetsu's studio Zonkoro, a large space that overlooks the pond, is now a multipurpose rental hall. Also available for hire are the three *chashitsu* in the garden: the adjoining pair Keijakuan and Isuitei (both built in 1932, the latter for the use of his wife Yone), and the thatch-roofed Mongyotei (built in 1924), suspended out over the water on the opposite side of the pond. Sadly, the former pair of tea houses was seriously damaged by fire in 2009, but the damage has since been repaired.

Above left The adjoining pair of tea houses, Keijakuan and Isuitei, were both built in 1932, the latter for the use of Kensetsu's wife Yone.

Above right The thatch-roofed Mongyotei pavilion, built in 1924, is suspended out over the water.

Right The rustic *tokonoma* alcove inside Isuitei.

Above Looking out at the pond from under the eaves of the ground floor room of Zonkoro.

Right A simple wooden gate located along one of the garden paths.

Far right A path through the lush planting of the garden. Kansetsu's attempts to improve his surroundings were not limited to his own estate. The hundreds of cherry blossom trees lining the nearby Philosopher's Path were planted by the artist and his wife, and are still known as "Kansetsu Sakura."

Kawai Kanjiro Memorial House

河井寛次郎記念館

LOCATION **HIGASHIYAMA-KU**
BUILT IN **1937**
ORIGINAL OWNER **KAWAI KANJIRO**

Above A ceramic artwork sitting in front of a *kakejiku* (hanging scroll) displaying the artist's own calligraphy, which reads "Folk Craft Study Collection."

Opposite The main room is a wood-floored, double-height space full of objects and furniture designed by Kanjiro. The table is piled with books about all the artists in the Mingei group, and the chair on the left is the work of British ceramic artist Bernard Leach (1887–1979).

The prolific artist Kawai Kanjiro (1890–1966) was one of the most famous exponents of Mingei, a folk art movement that attempted to revive the use of moribund vernacular styles, techniques, and materials. Comprising fellow artists Yanagi Soetsu, Hamada Shoji, Tomimoto Kenkichi, and Bernard Leach, the Mingei group mounted a quixotic challenge to the overwhelming increase in industrialized mass production that was indirectly causing the disappearance of traditional, everyday craft objects (though undeniably also making high-quality goods available to the general public). Emphasizing material qualities and the human touch, Mingei work is simultaneously handcraft and fine art—a distinction that has always been unclear in Japan. The Mingei movement has been criticized for its somewhat contrived romanticism, yet it was crucial in the preservation of skills that may have otherwise been forgotten.

Kanjiro is primarily known for his ceramic sculptures, but he often worked in wood in his later years and was a highly skilled calligrapher. He also designed his own home, used as both residence and atelier. Following Kanjiro's death in 1966, it was converted into a museum dedicated to his work, maintained by members of his family. A large collection of sculptures and other artworks are displayed throughout the rooms of the house, some using Kanjiro's distinctive motif of a stylized hand. Many more examples of his art may be found in the permanent collection of the National Museum of Modern Art in Kyoto. Famously, he never signed his work, and declined all official honors, including the prestigious designation of Living National Treasure. To the rear of the house is Kanjiro's kiln, called Shokeiyo, a *noborigama* (climbing kiln) comprising six chambers that step up the slope. Such kilns were once common in this area, and a few others survive. Indeed, it is the consummate skill of Kyoto's traditional ceramic artisans that engendered the high-tech ceramic industry thriving in present-day Kyoto.

Above left The various rooms of the house are now used as gallery spaces. Set on tatami mats against a backdrop of *fusuma* panels is a wooden sculpture using Kanjiro's distinctive hand motif.

Above right A display of art objects, many of them resulting from Kanjiro's experiments in ceramic glazing techniques, and some of the tools used to create them.

Left The rear corner of the house opens onto a generous courtyard garden.

Right above A former study, containing furniture and art works made by Kanjiro.

Far right above To the rear of the house is Shokeiyo, a *noborigama* (climbing kiln), which comprises six chambers that step up the slope.

Far right middle Samples from Kanjiro's endless experiments in ceramic glaze techniques.

試験用陶片
Test Pieces

Right Examples of Mingei-style ceramic and wood objects created by Kanjiro.

Below A detail of the swirling forms and varied materials that characterize the work of Mirei.

Right The garden visible from Kokokuan, a tea house also designed by Mirei and completed in 1969.

Shigemori Mirei Garden Museum

重森三玲庭園美術館

LOCATION **SAKYO-KU**

ESTABLISHED IN **1943**

ORIGINAL OWNER **SHIGEMORI MIREI**

Shigemori Mirei (1896–1975) remains Japan's most famous and influential modern garden designer, as well as having been a preeminent scholar on the history and techniques of Japanese garden design. After learning *chado* and ikebana as a teenager he studied *nihonga* (Japanese-style painting) at Tokyo University of the Arts, changing his given name from Kazuo to Mirei in homage to the French Realist painter Jean-François Millet (1814–75). He moved to Kyoto in 1929, first devoting his energy to ikebana then to a three-year nationwide survey of traditional gardens that resulted in a multivolume set of illustrated books, the last of which was published in 1938. That same year, Mirei received the commission that was to make him famous. The head priest of Tofuku-ji invited him to make an overall plan for the temple's future development, leading to Mirei's innovative and iconoclastic designs for the four gardens surrounding the *hojo* (abbot's quarters), which were completed in 1939. His work from that time onward was characterized by the use of elements previously unknown in Japanese gardens, including geometrical figures (straight lines and regular curves), modern materials such as concrete, and the use of unnatural colors.

Mirei's former residence is now a museum dedicated to his life and work, comprising an Edo Period machiya (built in 1789) that formerly belonged to the Suzuka family, hereditary retainers to the Yoshida family of nearby Yoshida Jinja shrine. Mirei purchased the house in 1943. He created two tea houses within the grounds, Mujian (1953) and Kokokuan (1969), along with fine examples of his own garden designs. The main garden, laid out in 1970, is in *karesansui* (dry landscape) style and contains four rock configurations symbolizing the Islands of the Immortals, one of Mirei's favorite themes. Compared to the aesthetically innovative designs Mirei produced elsewhere, it is a conservative composition, obviously intended to harmonize with the old house. Mirei is said to have enjoyed sitting at the east corner of the Shoin engawa gazing out across his own handiwork.

Above Softly separating the interior from the garden, *sudare* (reed blinds) hang from the eaves of Kokokuan.

Above Set in the garden in front of the Shoin, less than half of this distinctive boat-shaped stone is visible above ground.

Left above The main garden, laid out in 1970, is in *karesansui* (dry landscape) style and contains four rock configurations symbolizing the Islands of the Immortals, one of Mirei's favorite themes.

Left On the other side of the Shoin, adjacent to the *mizuya* (preparation room), this *tsuboniwa* (enclosed garden) was created in the 1960s and contains a number of salvaged and recycled objects.

Right Inside Kokokuan, a blue-and-white *ichimatsu* checkerboard pattern framed in wave shapes is spread across four *fusuma* panels.

Opposite below left A detail of the garden in front of Kokokuan.

Opposite below right The wooden gate leading to the front garden.

Shunki-an 旬季菴

LOCATION **MIYAMA-CHO**

BUILT IN **c.1700**

OWNERS **HIROSE MASANORI AND HIROSE MIYOKO**

Above To the right of the main house is a smaller building containing the bath.

Below The entrance gate is decorated with wild-flowers, and beyond is a *kayabuki* (thatch) roof in an *irimoya* (hipped and gabled) form.

Varying widely in style across the country according to the local climate and context, vernacular rural dwellings are predominantly defined by their roof forms, which may be broadly categorized into *kirizuma* (gabled), *yosemune* (hipped), and *irimoya* (hipped and gabled). Historically they tended to be clad in *kayabuki* (thatch) made of whatever was nearby: *susuki* (micanthus grass) in hilly areas, *yoshi* (ditch reed) in flat land, and barley straw when nothing else was available. Making them was a grueling task that involved the entire village, and they require rethatching every thirty years or so. The huge expense and effort involved, not to mention the fire hazard, have made them increasingly rare.

Located in the north part of Kyoto Prefecture, about 60 kilometers from the city, the Miyama-cho district is like a time warp: a serene rural setting for small villages containing *kayabuki* houses. Surrounded by mountains, traversed by the Yura River and the Sabakaido (Mackerel Road) that has connected Kyoto to the Japan Sea coast since the eighth century, the area contains about 250 *kayabuki* houses, most of them with irimoya style roofs. The highest concentration is to be found in Kitamura Village, also known as Kayabuki no Sato; of the fifty houses here, thirty-two have traditional *kayabuki* roofs. All of them date from the Edo period (1603–1867).

Although Kitamura is now an Important Traditional Building Preservation District, Shunki-an, formerly the residence of the leader of a local farming community, was not one of the houses to receive official protection and financial aid. In 1997 it was bought by Hirose Masanori, an Osaka restaurateur. He spent two years and a vast sum of money renovating it, coming from Osaka every weekend to supervise local carpenters. The house's lack of official protection allows it to be freely altered, and so the interior is full of unusual and innovative details, incorporating various antique objects collected by the owner.

Left At the center of the main living room is an *irori*, an open hearth set in the floor, used for warmth, light, and cooking in traditional rural houses. A metal *yakan* (kettle) hangs from an adjustable hook called a *jizaikagi*.

Below An eclectic mixture of furniture, paintings, decorative scrolls, and flower arrangements.

Bottom The corridor leading from the entry hall to the main living room.

Opposite above Traditional rural life centered on the *irori*, where guests were entertained, and meals were prepared and eaten.

Opposite below left One of the many examples of antique furniture placed throughout the house.

Opposite below center A home-cooked *sansai* (mountain vegetable) meal.

Opposite below right A row of *karakasa* (paper umbrellas).

Left A rough-hewn post, typical of rural dwellings.

Right Ikebana silhouetted against a *katomado* (flower-head window), a style of window imported from China and initially used only in Zen Buddhist temples.

Below Owner Hirose Miyoko tending the charcoal fire using a *hifukidake* bamboo pipe.

Above left A traditional squat toilet, lined with decorative stones and tiles.

Below A decorative lattice with a paper screen behind.

Above right The traditional-style bath has a view out to the garden.

Right A rustic guestroom containing a *byobu* (folding screen) covered with calligraphy.

Below A *kotatsu* (low wooden table skirted with a blanket, usually with a heater.

Right A secluded entry path to the rear entrance.

Right A wooden bench incorporating an old wagon wheel.

Far right An *onigawara* (decorative roof tile used at the end of a main ridge).

Suisen-an 粋仙庵

LOCATION **MIYAMA-CHO**

BUILT IN **c.1860**

OWNERS **AKIYAMA FUMIO AND AKIYAMA ETSUKO**

Above Of the fifty houses in Kitamura Village, thirty-two have painstakingly maintained *kayabuki* (thatched) roofs. The flowers in the foreground are *suisen* (Japanese daffodils).

Below The moss-covered roof of the Ishida House. Built in 1650, it is by far the oldest of the surviving *kayabuki* houses in this region.

Opposite Large picture windows provide a panoramic view over Miyama-cho, a superb natural landscape covered with forest and crossed by the Yura River.

Located near the west edge of rural Miyama-cho, the Ishida House is by far the oldest of the surviving *kayabuki* houses in this region. During dismantling and repair, a date was found inked on the structure confirming that it had been built in 1650. Uninhabited, it is now an officially designated Important Cultural Property maintained in an authentic state under the care of several elderly women living in the area. The style of the house is known as *kitayama*, with the entry in the gable end and the interior divided into a front half and rear half along the ridgeline of the *irimoya* roof. During the Edo Period (1603–1868) the Ishida family were leaders of the local village, and this area even today provides refuge from the cities for artisans intent on maintaining traditional craft techniques: ceramics, carpentry, lacquer work, gilding, fabric dyeing, *washi* paper making, and so on.

Not far from the Ishida House is Suisen-an, an exclusive country resort that opened in 2003 and only accepts one guest couple or family per night. The current owners, Akiyama Fumio and Etsuko, were both gymnastics teachers in Osaka who used to spend their family summer vacations in Miyama-cho, hoping to retire there. By chance they discovered Suisen-an, a 150-year-old *kayabuki* house without official protection, and were able to buy it in 1991, just before it was to be destroyed to make way for a new road. They had the house dismantled and moved to its present location, halfway up a hillside. It was then extended to create a space with picture windows open to spectacular panoramic views of the Miyama-cho landscape, covered with forests and crossed by the Yura River. Suisen-an has its own saké label, Miyama Suisen, brewed in nearby Kumihama by Philip Harper, a British-born resident who is the first foreigner to have ever attained the status of *toji* (master brewer).

Left Sitting on the veranda in front of the house is a portable charcoal brazier known as a *hibachi* (fire bowl), a traditional heating device that originated in China but has been used in Japan since at least the founding of Kyoto.

Below Despite the additions and alterations that have been made to the original house, the *irori* (open hearth set into the floor) remains the focus of daily life here.

Above An evening view of the dining room for guests, a warm space filled with an eclectic array of objects and furniture.

Right A daytime view of the dining room.

Far right An *itotsumugi* (spinning wheel) set in a corner.

tea houses

In 1587 Toyotomi Hideyoshi (1536–98), military ruler of Japan, hosted the largest tea ceremony in history: the Grand Kitano Tea Gathering. Announcements were posted all over Kyoto, making an open invitation to every tea aficionado who wished to attend, with the corollary that anyone who did not would be ostracized from the world of tea forever after. As many as 1500 temporary tea houses were assembled in the grounds of Kitano Shrine. Two extraordinary tea houses were central to the proceedings, one belonging to Hideyoshi and the other to his favored tea advisor Sen no Rikyu (1522–91). The former was an opulent portable pavilion that had been commissioned by Hideyoshi two years earlier, clad in gold leaf and lined with sheets of fine red silk. The latter was a humble, clay-walled, thatch-roofed hut, equally ostentatious in its overt display of poverty. While Hideyoshi took the opportunity to exhibit his enormous collection of valuable Chinese tea utensils as he served tea to his guests, Rikyu performed the *wabicha* tea ceremony with appropriate frugality and restraint. Thus the two extremes of tea house design were, for a brief moment, set side by side.

While the expressive possibilities cover the entire spectrum between them, it is the contrived rusticity of the *soan chashitsu* that is the model for most tea houses today. The typical tea house is a freestanding wooden pavilion set in a garden (though the word *chashitsu* may also refer to a room for the tea ceremony that is part of a larger structure), generally comprising two rooms: one for the ceremony and an adjacent room for preparation and storage called a *mizuya*. Opposite the tiny *nijiriguchi* entrance is a *tokonoma* alcove, which usually contains a *kakejiku* hanging scroll (during the first part of the ceremony) and an ikebana flower arrangement (during the second part of the ceremony). Every element in the room, from the *kakejiku* to the *chawan* (bowl), *kama* (kettle), and *chasen* (whisk) is selected to form an ensemble appropriate to the specific event.

Kodai-ji Shiguretei and Kasatei
高台寺

LOCATION **HIGASHIYAMA-KU**

BUILT IN **1606**

BUILT FOR **TOYOTOMI NENE**

Previous spread The *karesansui* (dry landscape) garden adjacent to the Tea Ceremony Hall of Urasenke.

Above The approach to the *kuri* (priests' quarters).

Below The doors of Chokushimon (Gate for Imperial Envoys).

Opposite above Called Hashintei (Waving Spirit Garden), the *karesansui* (dry landscape) garden in front of the *hojo* (abbot's quarters) is often used as a site for contemporary art installations.

Opposite below left Inside Garyoro (Reclining Dragon Corridor), the path that connects the mausoleum to the *kaisando* (Founder's Hall).

Opposite below right A distant view of the *kaisando*, in which the founding priest, Sanko Joeki (1572–1650), is enshrined.

Kodai-ji is a Rinzai Zen Buddhist temple established by Toyotomi Nene (1546–1624), the favorite wife of Toyotomi Hideyoshi (1536–98). When Hideyoshi was appointed *kanpaku*, making him senior advisor to the Emperor and de facto ruler of the nation, she received the aristocratic title Kita Mandokoro, the name by which she is now usually known. As was customary, she became a Buddhist nun after Hideyoshi's death, and went on to establish the temple Kodai-ji on the slopes of Mount Shuho, part of the Higashiyama mountain range at the east edge of Kyoto, where she resided for the rest of her life. The temple was intended as a memorial to Hideyoshi, who is interred there. Statues of Hideyoshi and Nene are on display in the mausoleum, one of the most highly decorated spaces to be found in the history of Japanese architecture.

At its height, Kodai-ji was a vast, thriving complex containing at least twelve subtemples, but three major fires in the late-eighteenth century destroyed all but a handful of the original structures. The majority of the land owned by Kodai-ji was officially confiscated during the Meiji Period, and it lost the status of a head temple, becoming a branch temple of nearby Kennin-ji temple. High on the slope on the east side of the temple, connected by an open sheltered walkway, are two of the surviving original structures: Kasatei (Umbrella Pavilion) and Shiguretei (Rainshower Pavilion), both now designated as Important Cultural Properties. It is often asserted that the pavilions were relocated from Fushimi Castle, Hideyoshi's residence during the secluded final few years of his life, and even that they were designed by Sen no Rikyu (1522–91). Though both have been used for tea ceremonies, they were created as multipurpose garden pavilions for all manner of festivities.

Above Ihoan (Memento Hut), a tea house characterized by a large circular window known as a *yoshi-no-mado*.

Right Shiguretei (Rainshower Pavilion), an unusual two-storied tea house design that was originally built for the Grand Kitano Tea Gathering of 1587. The covered walkway leads to the Kasatei tea house.

Below A mixture of materials used on the exterior walls of Kasatei.

Bottom left and right The bamboo ceiling structure below the *kayabuki* (thatch) roof may be glimpsed from outside.

Right Although its real name is Ankankutsu (Grotto of Idleness), this tea house is nicknamed Kasatei (Umbrella Hut) due to the resemblance of its bamboo-framed ceiling to a *karakasa* paper umbrella.

Toji-in 等持院

LOCATION **KITA-KU**

BUILT IN **1341**

BUILT FOR **ASHIKAGA TAKAUJI**

Originally named Kitatoji-ji at its founding in 1341 by Ashikaga Takauji (1305–58), Toji-in temple is the family temple of the Ashikaga shoguns, all fifteen of whom are buried here. The *hondo* (main hall) was built in 1616 as a *tatchu* (subtemple) of Myoshin-ji temple, and the garden is attributed to renowned landscape designer Muso Soseki (1275–1351). The eastern part of the garden is named Shinji-chi (Heart Pond) due to the resemblance of its pond to a cursive rendering of the kanji character *shin* 心 (heart). The western part is named Fuyo-chi (Lotus Pond), and Takauji's grave is set between the two ponds. The garden contains a spectacular array of flowering plants but, sadly, the *shakkei* (borrowed scenery) of nearby Mount Kinugasa has now been obscured by some of the buildings on the Ritsumeikan University campus.

Beside the lotus pond and north of the *hondo* is a small tea house called Seirentei (Pavilion of Pure Ripples), originally built by the eighth Ashikaga shogun, Yoshimasa (1435–90). The exterior has the appearance of a *soan chashitsu* with a *kayabuki* (thatched) roof in a *yosemune* (hipped) form, and the interior comprises an unusual layout of four tatami mats. The *jodan* (raised floor) tatami mat is a *daimedatami* (three-quarter size mat), in order to accommodate the *tokonoma* alcove, which is oriented sideways. Directly above the *jodan* is an *ajiro* (wickerwork) ceiling, and behind it is a window containing two shoji screens with a curving wooden lintel. Attached to the west side of Seirentei is a *chashitsu* with a conventional *yojohan* (four and a half tatami mat) plan and a *kirizuma* (gabled) roof. The two structures are linked by a *mizuya* (preparation and storage room). Interestingly, the famous *Miyako Rinsen Meisho Zue* (Illustrated Guide to Famous Places in Kyoto), a multi-volume book published in 1799 by poet Akisato Rito (1776–1830), shows Seirintei without the *mizuya* or the *yojohan* annex, suggesting that it was originally intended as simply a pavilion for looking at the view.

Above A view of the *hondo* (main hall).

Below This later addition to Seirentei (Pavilion of Pure Ripples) is a tea house with a conventional *yojohan* (four and a half tatami mat) plan and a *kirizuma* (gabled) roof.

Opposite Viewed across Fuyo-chi (Lotus Pond), the *hondo* is to the left and Seirentei to the right. Built by the eighth Ashikaga shogun, Yoshimasa (1435–90), Seirentei is a *soan chashitsu* (rustic tea house) with a *kayabuki* (thatched) roof.

Above Seirentei has unusual proportions due to its four tatami-mat interior layout. The *mizuya* (preparation and storage room) and *yojohan* annex may be glimpsed to the rear.

Opposite above left Inside Seirentei, the *jodan* (raised floor) tatami mat is a *daimedatami* (three-quarter size mat), in order to accommodate the *tokonoma* alcove, which is oriented sideways.

Above A detail of the Seirentei annex.

Below Visible above the *jodan* is an *ajiro* (wicker-work) ceiling, and behind it is a window containing two shoji screens with a curving lintel.

Daitoku-ji Koto-in Shoko-ken

高桐院

LOCATION **KITA-KU**

BUILT IN **1628**

BUILT FOR **HOSOKAWA TADAOKI**

Above The stone-paved *sando* (approach route) leading to Koto-in passes through bamboo thickets.

Opposite above A view of Ihokuken, a building relocated here in 1602 from the residence of Sen no Rikyu (1522–91).

Opposite below left Omotemon (Front Gate).

Opposite below right The third gate of the extended entry sequence to the temple.

Shoko-ken is a *nijodaime* (two-and-three-quarter tatami mat) *sukiya* tea house located within the grounds of Koto-in, one of the smaller subtemples of Daitoku-ji Temple. Koto-in was established in 1601 by Hosokawa Tadaoki (1563–1646), a prominent aristocrat, aesthete, and military leader. A devotee of the tea ceremony from an early age, he became a student of Sen no Rikyu (1522–91) and took the Buddhist name Sansai. In 1621 he retired from public life and devoted himself to tea. As one of Rikyu's seven main disciples, their relationship was very close: when Rikyu was ordered to commit ritual suicide, Sansai provided one of his own retainers as *kaishaku* (the person entrusted with the task of making the final decapitation), and later became patron and employer of Rikyu's son, Doan.

Attached to the northeast corner of Koto-in's main building, Shoko-ken is one of several tea houses designed by Sansai himself (and originally created for the Grand Kitano Tea Gathering of 1587) but is believed to be the only authentic example still standing. In the history of tea, Sansai tends to be regarded as an orthodox adherent of Rikyu's style, overshadowed by his more innovative peer Furuta Oribe (1545–1615). Indeed, the layout of Shoko-ken is very similar to *nijodaime* tea houses designed by Rikyu.

There is a tragic side to Sansai's retreat into the world of tea. His wife Tama (1563–1600) had been interested in the new religion of Christianity, introduced to Japan during the sixteenth century. In 1587 Toyotomi Hideyoshi (1536–98) issued an edict forbidding Christianity and expelling the Jesuit missionaries, inspiring Tama to have herself secretly—and riskily—baptized, taking the Christian name Gracia. She was killed (or possibly committed suicide to avoid capture) during the battles for power that followed Hideyoshi's death, and is rumored to have been canonized by the Vatican in 1862. Sansai and Gracia are both interred at Koto-in.

Above A broad corridor inside Ihokuken.

Above left The interior of the Kyakuden (Reception Hall).

Above right Looking out to the garden from the Kyakuden.

Below The calligraphy on this *kakejiku* (hanging scroll) reads *ittei san ko yu* ("a single chirp deepens the silence of the mountain").

Right The *wabi sabi* atmosphere of a room inside Ihokuken.

Above The Shokoken tea house, designed by Hoso-kawa Tadaoki (1563–1646). The irregularly shaped red pine *tokobashira* is original, but almost every other element has been replaced over the centuries.

Right The Kyakuden shrouded in greenery.

Right The broad moss garden to the south of the Kyakuden contains a single *toro* (stone lantern). Comprising wooden planks with their crosscut ends exposed, the *engawa* is a type known as a *kirime-en*.

Below left A *takesunoko-en* (veranda made of bamboo rods).

Below center Stepping stones leading into the garden.

Below right A small *takegaki* (bamboo fence).

Murin-an 無鄰菴

LOCATION **SAKYO-KU**

BUILT IN **1896**

ORIGINAL OWNER **YAMAGATA ARITOMO**

Above The expansive estate combines aspects of the traditional Japanese *kaiyushiki teien* (stroll garden) and the broad lawns of the English landscape garden.

Below A view of the garden from the veranda of the *sukiya*-style *omoya* (main wing of the house).

Opposite The two-story residence combines aspects of Western and Japanese architecture. The Higashiyama mountains visible in the distance have been incorporated into the design of the garden, a fine example of *shakkei* (borrowed scenery).

Born into a samurai family, Yamagata Aritomo (1838–1922) was a controversial Meiji Period statesman. He and members of his family were central figures in the 1866 revolution against the Tokugawa Shogunate that led to the return of the Emperor to power in 1868, an event now known as the Meiji Restoration. Aritomo received a noble title as a consequence, and went on to hold various political and military titles. Appointed War Minister in 1873 and Lord Chancellor in 1883, he was Prime Minister of Japan from 1889 to 1891. He was a Commanding General during the First Sino-Japanese War (1894–5), receiving the rank of Field Marshal in 1898, and was elected to a second term as Prime Minister that same year. Aritomo was instrumental in instigating the Russo-Japanese War (1904–5), during which he was again a Commanding General. Deeply conservative in ideology and policy, he is considered a key influence on the increasing militarization that culminated in Japan's entry into the Second World War.

Yet, Aritomo was also a respected aesthete. Murin-an, his second residence, now owned by the Kyoto municipality, is highly regarded, particularly due to the garden he created in collaboration with Ogawa Jihei (1860–1932), one of Kyoto's most famous garden designers. The two-story *sukiya*-style house manifests a Western influence, prevalent among aristocratic dwellings during that period, as does the garden with its large areas of lawn. Containing a *sanjodaime* (three and three-quarter tatami mat) tea house, the garden is a *kaiyushiki teien* (stroll garden) based around branching streams and ponds that converge in front of the main house. The design of the garden makes good use of a technique known as *miegakure*, in which elements set within the garden are sequentially hidden and revealed from different angles. It is also an excellent example of *shakkei* (borrowed scenery), incorporating the distant scenery by means of two groves of trees that frame a part of the Higashiyama mountain range.

Above Viewed here from the *omoya*, the tea house is an imitation of the Ennan tea house designed by Furuta Oribe (1545–1615), a student of Sen no Rikyu (1522–91). Ennan is the property of Yabunouchi-ryu, one of the four main tea ceremony schools in Kyoto.

Right Rich green moss carpets much of the garden.

Left The veranda on the right provides a good vantage point for looking out at the mountains. To the left is the *sanjo-daime* (three and three-quarter tatami mat) tea house itself.

Below left A detail of the shoji windows inside the tea house.

Below right Rich and complex spaces are contained in the compact volume.

Shokado Garden Art Museum
松花堂庭園・美術館

LOCATION **YAWATA-SHI**
ESTABLISHED IN **1637**
ORIGINAL OWNER **SHOKADO SHOJO**

Above The cobblestone path to the Shoin, passing Shokado *soan chashitsu* on the left-hand side. Both buildings have been relocated here from the Izuminobo temple on Mount Otoko.

Nakanuma Shikibu (1582–1639), usually known as Shokado Shojo, was a Buddhist priest widely admired for his talents in painting, poetry, ikebana, and the art of tea. Considered one of the greatest calligraphers of the Kan'ei Era (1624–44), he is founder of the Shokado style of calligraphy. At the age of sixteen, Shojo became an acolyte at Iwashimizu Hachimangu, a Shinto shrine located at the top of Mount Otoko, southwest of Kyoto. At that time the shrine was designated Ryobu Shinto, a synthesis of the native Japanese religion with imported Shingon Buddhism, based on the belief that Shinto deities were manifestations of Buddhist divinities. Shojo was eventually appointed head of the Takimotobo subtemple in 1627, but when a major fire damaged the building ten years later, he passed his position on to a disciple and built himself a *soan chashitsu* called Shokado (Pine Flower Hall) in the grounds of the nearby Izuminobo subtemple. Well acquainted with the artists and intellectuals of the age, such as regent Konoe Nobuhiro (1599–1649), tea master Kobori Enshu (1579–1647), poet Ishikawa Jozan (1583–1672), and Confucian philosopher Hayashi Razan (1583–1657), he turned Shokado into a famed literary salon and venue for tea ceremonies.

As part of the government suppression of Buddhism in the early Meiji Period, all the temples on Mount Otoko were dismantled and sold, and Iwashimizu Hachimangu became a purely Shinto shrine. Shojo's *soan chashitsu* was moved down from the mountain and rebuilt in the inner garden of what is now the Shokado Garden Art Museum. The inner garden contains a *karesansui* (dry landscape) garden and a *kokeniwa* (moss garden) together with a Shoin hall also relocated from Izuminobo. Surrounding this area is a large outer garden containing many types of camellia and bamboo, as well as three other *chashitsu*, one of which is a reproduction of a design by tea master Kobori Enshu (1579–1647).

Left The entrance gate to the inner garden, as seen from Shokado.

Below left The rear of Shokado, seen through the trees of the inner garden.

Below right The austere composition of Shokado's interior, comprising tatami mats and unadorned *fusuma* panels.

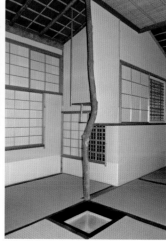

Top left Kanunken, a *chashitsu* located in the outer garden. This is a replica of a design by famed tea master Kobori Enshu (1579–1647).

Top right Inside Kanunken, the rectilinear arrangement of shoji panels is offset by the naturally twisted form of the *tokobashira* post.

Above The entry to the Shoin.

Right An idiosyncratically paved path, set alongside a small stream that flows toward the entrance gate.

Above Baiinseki, a *chashitsu* located in the outer garden.

Right The Shoin in the inner garden, with the long branch of a pine tree in the foreground.

Urasenke 裏千家

LOCATION **KAMIGYO-KU**

BUILT IN **1642 / CHADO KAIKAN IN 1956**

BUILT FOR **SEN SOTAN**

Above The *roji* garden path leading from the street gate to the entrance foyer of the historical Konnichian estate.

Opposite above Looking through a bamboo fence to the austere *karesansui* (dry landscape) garden adjacent to the Chado Kaikan, a two-story building located directly opposite the entrance to Konnichian.

Opposite below left Kabutomon (Helmet Gate), marking the street entry to Konnichian, was built during the nineteenth century by Gengensai Seichu Soshitsu (1810–77), the eleventh-generation *iemoto*.

Opposite below right The entry to the Konnichian tea room complex. The stepping stones of the *roji* path end at an area of diamond-shaped tiles and a wide wooden step in front of the *genkan*. A low wall to the left separates the main entrance from a smaller, secondary entrance.

Though certainly not the sole originator, tea master Sen no Rikyu (1522–91) was hugely influential on the form of the tea ceremony as it exists today. A prodigy and iconoclast, as his fame increased he became an advisor to Oda Nobunaga (1534–82), the samurai lord who began the process of reunifying Japan after a long period of civil war. With Nobunaga's death, his successor Toyotomi Hideyoshi (1537–98) inherited his rights and responsibilities together with a select group of tea advisors that included Rikyu. Though Rikyu became a favored and trusted confidante, for reasons unknown he eventually incurred Hideyoshi's wrath and was ordered to commit ritual suicide. This no doubt gave great pleasure to Rikyu's many jealous enemies, temporarily ruining his posthumous reputation and shaming his family—it was not until a decade later that his grandson, Sen no Sotan (1578–1658), was given official permission to restore the Senke (Sen family) within Kyoto society. Sotan trained his three sons (Soshitsu, Sosa, and Soshu) in the tea arts and each became the progenitor of an independent tea school: Urasenke, Omotesenke, and Mushakojisenke. Though all three lineages are active today, it is Urasenke that has the highest profile, establishing international branches and welcoming interested students from all over the world. The head of a hereditary guild such as a tea school is known as the *iemoto*, and each carries the founder's name. Now at the sixteenth generation, Urasenke's current *iemoto* is Zabosai Genmoku Soshitsu.

The core of the Urasenke estate is the *chashitsu* built by Sen no Sotan for his retirement, known as Konnichi-an (Hermitage of This Day). Various other structures are now spread throughout the garden, including the Yuin and Kan'untei tea houses and an ancestral shrine dedicated to Rikyu. The entire complex was designated an Important Cultural Property in 1976. Located across the street is the Chado Kaikan, completed in 1956 and now used for lessons and seminars. The ground level contains three tearooms, called Shinka (Heart Flower), Houn (Phoenix Cloud), and Kasho (Auspicious Pine).

Far left The *ichimatsu* (checkerboard) patterns of the *fusuma* panels in Shinka (Flower of the Heart), one of the three tea rooms inside the Chado Kaikan.

Left A view of the garden from Shinka.

Left below Houn (Phoenix Cloud), another of the tea rooms inside the Chado Kaikan.

Right A view into the Houn tea room from the adjacent space.

Below left The *tokonoma* alcove in the Shinka tea room.

Below center A bamboo water feature in the Chado Kaikan garden.

Below right A *koshikake* (waiting bench) in the Konnichian garden.

Daitoku-ji Juko-in Kan'inseki Masudokoseki

大徳寺 聚光院

LOCATION **KITA-KU**

BUILT IN **1566**

ORIGINAL OWNER **MIYOSHI YOSHITSUGU**

Above The path of stepping stones leading into the garden adjacent to Kan'inseki.

Opposite The *karesansui* (dry landscape) garden on the south side of the *hojo* (main hall) is believed to have been laid out by Sen no Rikyu (1522–91) based on a design by the painter Kano Eitoku (1543–90).

Juko-in temple contains the setting for one of the defining moments in the cultural history of Kyoto: the ritual suicide of famed tea master Sen no Rikyu (1522–91) at the order of Toyotomi Hideyoshi (1536–98). Though this event actually took place in a small *chashitsu* (tea house) called Kan'inseki that was located at Rikyu's own residence, a replica of the space was created at Juko-in in 1741, the 150th anniversary of Rikyu's death—a gift from Omotesenke, one of the three tea schools maintained by Rikyu's descendants (the other two are Urasenke and Mushakojisenke). Only three tatami mats in area, Kan'inseki reflects Rikyu's preference for maximum simplicity and austerity. The adjacent garden contains two of Rikyu's prized possessions, a stone lantern and stone washbasin. Kan'inseki has since been incorporated into a larger structure, which contains a second *chashitsu*, also donated by Omotesenke, called Masudoko-no-seki. The two *chashitsu* are separated by a *mizuya* (preparation room), and the different eras of design and construction are visible in the changing heights of the lintels across the interior walls.

A Rinzai Zen subtemple of Daitoku-ji temple, Juko-in was established in 1566 as a memorial to samurai lord Miyoshi Nagayoshi (1523–64) by his nephew (and later adopted son) Miyoshi Yoshitsugu (1549–73). The first abbot was Shorei Sokin (1505–83), the tea master who taught Rikyu. Sokin's grave is located in the temple graveyard, as is a stone pagoda supposedly marking Rikyu's grave—though with two other gravesites for Rikyu elsewhere, the true location of his earthly remains is unknown. Nevertheless, two years before his death Rikyu had designated Juko-in to be his family temple, and each successive *iemoto* (hereditary head) of the three Senke tea schools is buried in the temple graveyard. Juko-in remains central to the Kyoto tea world: every month, one of the Senke schools holds a memorial service here for Rikyu.

Above Looking toward the alcove of Kan'inseki, a *chashitsu* that is only three tatami mats in area, with a view through to the *mizuya* (preparation room) on the right.

Left Looking out from Kan'in-seki to the tea garden, which contains two of Sen no Rikyu's (1522–91) prized possessions—a stone lantern and stone washbasin.

Left The tea garden adjacent to Kan'inseki.

Right Masudoko-no-seki, a *chashitsu* named for its *masudoko*, a half-tatami sized *tokonoma* alcove contained by a half-height wall.

Bibliography

Adolphson, Mikael S. (2000). *The Gates of Power: Monks, Courtiers, and Warriors in Premodern Japan*. Honolulu: University of Hawaii Press.

Alex, William (1965). *Japanese Architecture*. London: Prentice-Hall International.

Berque, Augustin (1997). *Japan: Nature, Artifice and Japanese Culture*. Northhamptonshire: Pilkington Press.

Blaser, Werner (1956). *Japanese Temples and Tea-Houses*. New York: F. W. Dodge Corporation.

Brown, Kendall H. (1997). *The Politics of Reclusion: Painting and Power in Momoyama Japan*. Honolulu: University of Hawaii Press.

Clancy, Judith (1997). *Exploring Kyoto: On Foot in the Ancient Capital*. New York: Weatherhill.

Coaldrake, William H. (1996). *Architecture and Authority in Japan*. London: Routledge Japanese Studies Series.

Drexler, Arthur (1955). *The Architecture of Japan*. New York: Museum of Modern Art.

Durston, Diane (1986). *Old Kyoto: A Guide to Traditional Shops, Restaurants, and Inns*. Tokyo: Kodansha International.

Durston, Diane (1987). *Kyoto: Seven Paths to the Heart of the City*. Tokyo: Kodansha International.

Enders, Siegfried RCT (1999). *Hozon: Architectural and Urban Conservation in Japan*. Baden-Württemberg: Edition Axel Menges.

Engel, Heino (1985). *Measure and Construction of the Japanese House*. New York: Tuttle.

Hirai, Kiyosi (1998). *The Japanese House Then and Now* (Martie Jelinek, Trans.). Tokyo: Ichigaya Publications.

Horiguchi, Sutemi; Kojiro, Yuichiro, & Hamaguchi, Ryuichi (1956). *Architectural Beauty in Japan*. Tokyo: Kokusai Bunka Shinkokai.

Inoue, Mitsuo (1985). *Space in Japanese Architecure* (Hiroshi Watanabe, Trans.). New York: Weatherhill.

Isozaki, Arata (2006). *Japan-ness in Architecture* (Sabu Kohso, Trans.). Cambridge: MIT Press.

Kawashima, Chuji (1986). *Minka: Traditional Houses of Rural Japan* (Lynne E. Riggs, Trans.). Tokyo: Kodansha International.

Keene, Donald (2003). *Yoshimasa and the Silver Pavilion: The Creation of the Soul of Japan*. New York: Columbia University Press.

Kurokawa, Kisho (1988). *Rediscovering Japanese Space*. New York: Weatherhill.

Larsen, Knut Einar (1994). *Architectural Preservation in Japan*. Trondheim: Tapir/ICOMOS.

Levine, Gregory P. A. (2006). *Daitokuji: The Visual Cultures of a Zen Monastery*. Washington: University of Washington Press.

Mishima, Yukio (2001). *The Temple of the Golden Pavilion*. New York: Vintage.

Naito, Akira, & Nishikawa, Takeshi (1977). *Katsura: A Princely Retreat* (Charles S. Terry, Trans.). New York: Kodansha.

Nakagawa, Takeshi (2005). *The Japanese House in Space, Memory, and Language* (Geraldine Harcourt, Trans.). Tokyo: I-House Press.

Nishi, Kazuo, & Hozumi, Kazuo (1996). *What is Japanese Architecture? A Survey of Traditional Japanese Architecture*. Tokyo: Kodansha International.

Okakura, Kakuzo (2006). *The Book of Tea*. Tokyo: Kodansha.

Pitelka, Morgan (2003). *Japanese Tea Culture: Art, History and Practice*. London: Routledge Curzon.

Plutschow, Herbert E. (1983). *Historical Kyoto*. Tokyo: The Japan Times.

Richie, Donald (1995). *The Temples of Kyoto*. New York: Tuttle.

Rimer, J. Thomas; Chaves, Jonathan; Addiss, Stephen, & Suzuki, Hiroyuki (1991). *Shisendo: Hall of the Poetry Immortals*. New York: Weatherhill.

Sadler, Arthur L. (1962). *A Short History of Japanese Architecture*. Tokyo: Charles E. Tuttle Company.

Sadler, Arthur L. (2001). *Cha-No-Yu: The Japanese Tea Ceremony*. Tokyo: Tuttle.

Stavros, Matthew (2015). *Kyoto: An Urban History of Japan's Premodern Capital*. Honolulu: University of Hawaii Press.

Tange, Kenzo; Gropius, Walter, & Ishimoto, Yasuhiro (1960). *Katsura: Tradition and Creation in Japanese Architecture*. New Haven, London: Yale University Press.

Tanizaki, Junichiro (1977). *In Praise of Shadows* (Thomas J. Harper and Edward G. Seidensticker, Trans.). Tokyo: Tuttle Publishing.

Taut, Bruno (1936). *Fundamentals of Japanese Architecture*. Tokyo: Kokusai Bunka Shinkokai.

Taut, Bruno (1937). *Houses and People of Japan*. Tokyo: Gridford-Sanseidô.

Treib, Marc, & Herman, Ron (2003). *A Guide to the Gardens of Kyoto*. Tokyo: Kodansha International.

Tschumi, Christian (2005). *Mirei Shigemori: Modernizing the Japanese Garden*. Berkeley: Stone Bridge Press.

Ueda, Atsushi (1998). *The Inner Harmony of the Japanese House*. Tokyo: Kodansha International.

Van Goethem, Ellen (2008). *Nagaoka: Japan's Forgotten Capital*. Leiden: Brill.

Varley, Paul, & Isao, Kumakura (Eds.) (1989). *Tea in Japan: Essays on the History of Chanoyu*. Honolulu: University of Hawaii Press.

Waley, Paul, & Fieve, Nicholas (Eds.) (2003). *Japanese Capitals in Historical Perspective: Place, Power and Memory in Kyoto, Edo and Tokyo*. London: Curzon.

Wheatley, Paul, & See, Thomas (1978). *From Court to Capital: A Tentative Interpretation of the Origins of the Japanese Urban Tradition*. Chicago: University of Chicago Press.

Zeami (2006). *The Flowering Spirit: Classic Teachings on the Art of No* (William Scott Wilson, Trans.). Tokyo: Kodansha International.

List of Houses and Gardens

Aristocratic Villas

Katsura Imperial Villa 桂離宮
Katsuramisono Nishigyo-ku Kyoto-shi
京都市西京区桂御園
Tel: 075-211-1215
sankan.kunaicho.go.jp/guide/katsura.html

Shugakuin Imperial Villa 修学院離宮
Shuugakuin Yabusoe Sakyo-ku Kyoto-shi
京都市左京区修学院藪添
Tel: 075-211-1215
sankan.kunaicho.go.jp/guide/shugakuin.html

Kyoto Imperial Palace 京都御所
Kyoto Gyoennai Kamigyo-ku Kyoto-shi
京都市上京区京都御苑内
Tel: 075-211-1215
sankan.kunaicho.go.jp/guide/kyoto.html

Daikaku-ji 大覚寺
Saga-Osawa-cho Ukyo-ku Kyoto-shi
京都市右京区嵯峨大沢町4
Tel: 075-871-0071
www.daikakuji.or.jp

Byodo-in 平等院
116 Uji-renge Uji-shi Kyoto-fu
京都府宇治市宇治蓮華116
Tel: 0774-21-2861
www.byodoin.or.jp

Kinkaku-ji 金閣寺
1 Kinkaku-ji-cho Kita-ku Kyoto
京都市北区金閣寺町1
Tel: 075-461-0013
www.shokoku-ji.or.jp/kinkakuji/index.html

Ginkaku-ji 銀閣寺
Ginkaku-ji-cho Sakyo-ku Kyoto-shi
京都市左京区銀閣寺町2
Tel: 075-771-5725
www.shokoku-ji.or.jp/ginkakuji/index.html

Jakko-in 寂光院
676 Oharakusao-cho Sakyo-ku Kyoto-shi
京都市左京区大原草生町676
Tel: 075-861-1769
www.jakkoin.jp

Temple Residences

Ryogen-in 大徳寺 龍源院
82-1 Murasakino Daitokuji-cho Kita-ku Kyoto-shi
京都市北区紫野大徳寺町82-1
Tel: 075-491-7635

Shoren-in 青蓮院門跡
69-1 Awadaguchi Sanjobo-cho Higashiyama-ku Kyoto-shi
京都市東山区粟田口三条坊町69-1
Tel: 075-561-2345

Tofuku-ji 東福寺
15-778 Honmachi Higashiyama-ku Kyoto-shi
京都市東山区本町15-778
Tel: 075-561-0087

Ryogin-an 東福寺 龍吟庵
15-812 Honmachi Higashiyama-ku Kyoto-shi
京都市東山区本町15-812
Tel: 075-561-0087

Ninna-ji 仁和寺
33 Omuro Ouchi Ukyo-ku Kyoto-shi
京都市右京区御室大内33
Tel: 075-461-1155
www.ninnaji.or.jp

Nanzen-ji 南禅寺
86 Nanzenji Fukuchi-cho Sakyo-ku Kyoto-shi
京都市左京区南禅寺福地町86
Tel: 075-771-0365
www.nanzen.net

Kanchi-in 東寺 観智院
403 Kujo-cho Hachijo Omiyanishi-iru Minami-ku Kyoto-shi
京都市南区八条大宮西入ル九条町403
Tel: 075-691-1131

Jingo-ji 高雄山 神護寺
5 Takao-cho Umegahata Ukyo-ku Kyoto-shi
京都市右京区梅ケ畑高雄町5
Tel: 075-861-1769
www.jingoji.org

Merchant Townhouses

Kinpyo 金瓢
335 Miyoshi-cho Furumonzen Higashiyama-ku Kyoto-shi
京都市東山区吉門前通三吉町335
Tel: 075-561-1550
www.kinpyo.jp

Kinmata 近又
Gokomachi Shijo-agaru Nakagyo-ku Kyoto-shi
京都市中京区御幸町四条上ル
Tel: 075-221-1039
www.kinmata.com

Inakatei 田舎亭
463 Ishibei-koji Gion Shitakawara Higashiyama-ku Kyoto-shi
京都市東山区祇園下河原石塀小路463
Tel: 075-561-3059
www.inakatei.com

Iori Minoya-cho 庵 美濃屋町
Kiyamachi-dori Matsubara-agaru Shimogyo-ku Kyoto-shi
京都市下京区木屋町通松原上ル
Tel: 075-352-0211
www.kyoto-machiya.com

Iori Sujiya-cho 庵 筋屋町
Tominokoji-dori Takatsuji-agaru Shimogyo-ku Kyoto-shi
京都市下京区富小路通高辻上ル
Tel: 075-352-0211
www.kyoto-machiya.com

Iori Zaimoku-cho 庵 材木町
Kiyamachi-dori Matsubara-sagaru Shimogyo-ku
Kyoto-shi
京都市下京区木屋町通松原下ル
Tel: 075-352-0211
www.kyoto-machiya.com

Iori Sanbo Nishinotoin-cho
庵 三坊西洞院町
Nishinotoin-dori Oike-sagaru Nakagyo-ku Kyoto-
shi
京都市中京区西洞院通御池下ル
Tel: 075-352-0211
www.kyoto-machiya.com

Traditional Inns

Hiiragiya 柊家
Nakahakusan-cho Fuya-cho Anekoji-agaru
Nakagyo-ku Kyoto-shi
京都市中京区麩屋町姉小路上ル中白山町
Tel: 075-221-1136
www.hiiragiya.co.jp

Gion Hatanaka 祇園 畑中
Yasaka Jinja Minamimonmae Higashiyama-ku
Kyoto-shi
京都市東山区祇園八坂神社南門前
Tel: 075-541-5315
www.thehatanaka.co.jp

Rangetsu 嵐月
7 Saga Tenryuji Susukinobaba-cho Ukyo-ku
Kyoto-shi
京都市右京区嵯峨天龍寺芒ノ馬場町7
Tel: 075-865-2000
www.rangetsu.jp

Jijuden 仁寿殿ゲストハウス京都
1 Somon-cho Kinugasa Kita-ku Kyoto-shi
京都市北区衣笠総門町1
Tel: 075-466-2112
www.jijuden.com

Momijiya もみち 家
Takao Umegahata Ukyo-ku Kyoto-shi
京都市右京区梅ケ畑高雄
Tel: 075-871-1005
www.jijuden.com

Yoshida Sanso 吉田山荘
59-1 Yoshida Shimo-oji-cho Sakyo-ku,
京都市左京区吉田下大路町59-1
Tel: 075-771-6125
www.yoshidasanso.com

Miyamaso 美山荘
Daihizan Hanaseharachi Sakyo-ku Kyoto-shi
京都市左京区花背原地町大悲山
Tel: 075-746-0231
www.miyamasou.co.jp

Private Retreats

Shisendo 詩仙堂
27 Kadoguchi-cho Ichijoji Sakyo-ku Kyoto-shi
京都市左京区一乗寺門口町27
Tel: 075-781-2954
www.kyoto-shisendo.com

Okouchi Sanso 大河内山荘
8 Yamatabuchiyama-cho Sagaogura Ukyo-ku
Kyoto-shi
京都市右京区嵯峨小倉山田渕山町 8
Tel: 075-872-2233

Hakusasonso 橋本関雪記念館
37 Jodoji Ishibashi-cho Sakyo-ku Kyoto-shi
京都市左京区浄土寺石橋町37
Tel: 075-751-0446
www.kansetsu.or.jp

Kawai Kanjiro Memorial House
河井寛次郎記念館
569 Gojozaka Kanei-cho Higashiyama-ku Kyoto-shi
京都市東山区五条坂鐘鋳町569
Tel: 075-561-3585
http://hcn.plala.or.jp/fc211/sagi

Shigemori Mirei Garden Museum
重森三玲庭園美術館
34 Yoshidakami-oji-cho Sakyo-ku, Kyoto-shi
京都市左京区吉田上大路町34
Tel: 075-761-8776
www.est.hi-ho.ne.jp/shigemori

Shunki-an 旬季菴
4-2 Higashida Mitsuno Miyama-cho Nantan Kyoto-fu
京都府南丹市美山町三埜東田 4-2
Tel: 0771-75-0353

Suisen-an 粋仙庵
81-1 Oharadani Kashihara Miyama-cho Nantan
Kyoto-fu
京都府南丹市美山町樫原大原谷81-1
Tel: 0771-75-1625
www.suisen-an.com

Tea Houses

Kodai-ji 高台寺
526 Shimokawara-cho Kodaiji Higashiyama-ku
Kyoto-shi
京都市東山区高台寺下河原町526
Tel: 075-561-9966
www.kodaiji.com

Toji-in 等持院
63 Kitamachi Toji-in Kita-ku Kyoto-shi
京都市北区等持院北町63
Tel: 075-461-5786

Daitoku-ji Koto-in Shoko-ken 高桐院
73-1 Murasakino Daitokuji-cho Kita-ku Kyoto-shi
京都市北区紫野大徳寺町73-1
Tel: 075-492-0068

Murin-an 無鄰菴
31 Kusagawa-cho Nanzenji Sakyo-ku Kyoto-shi
京都市左京区南禅寺草川町31
Tel: 075-771-3909

Shokado Garden Art Museum
松花堂庭園・美術館
43 Yawata Ominaeshi Yawata-shi Kyoto-fu
京都府八幡市八幡女郎花43
Tel: 075-981-0010
www.yawata-bunka.jp/syokado/index.htm

Urasenke 裏千家
613 Honpojimae-cho Ogawa Teranouchi-agaru
Kamigyo-ku Kyoto-shi
京都市上京区本法寺前町613
Tel: 075-431-3111
www.urasenke.or.jp

Daitoku-ji Juko-in Kan'inseki Masudokoseki
大徳寺 聚光院
58 Murasakino Daitokuji-cho Kita-ku Kyoto-shi
京都市北区紫野大徳寺町58
Tel: 075-492-6880

Acknowledgments

I would like to extend my sincere thanks to the owners, managers, and staff of all the ryokan, machiya, country retreats, temples, and historical homes featured in this book. They provided us with great support, and without their assistance and cooperation it would not have been possible to bring this book to fruition.

I also extend heartiest appreciation to my wife Asako, who spent a great deal of time with me during photo shoots, acting as my assistant, coordinator, and sometimes design supervisor.

A special thank you also goes to Thomas Daniell, who wrote the text with the eyes of an architect, as well as to publisher Eric Oey, editorial supervisor June Chong, and designer Chan Sow Yun of Tuttle Publishing, who all put a lot of effort into this publication.

Akihiko (Alan) Seki

About Tuttle
"Books to Span the East and West"

Our core mission at Tuttle Publishing is to create books which bring people together one page at a time. Tuttle was founded in 1832 in the small New England town of Rutland, Vermont (USA). Our fundamental values remain as strong today as they were then—to publish best-in-class books informing the English-speaking world about the countries and peoples of Asia. The world has become a smaller place today and Asia's economic, cultural and political influence has expanded, yet the need for meaningful dialogue and information about this diverse region has never been greater. Since 1948, Tuttle has been a leader in publishing books on the cultures, arts, cuisines, languages and literatures of Asia. Our authors and photographers have won numerous awards and Tuttle has published thousands of books on subjects ranging from martial arts to paper crafts. We welcome you to explore the wealth of information available on Asia at **www.tuttlepublishing.com**.

Published by Tuttle Publishing, an imprint of Periplus Editions (HK) Ltd

www.tuttlepublishing.com

Photographs copyright © 2017 Akihiko Seki
Text copyright © 2017 Thomas Daniell
All photographs by Akihiko Seki except page 10, courtesy of Urasenke/
Tanko-sha, and page 57 © iStockphoto.com/cOmOtiOn

ISBN: 978-4-8053-1471-5
(*Previously published under ISBN 978-4-8053-1091-5*)

Distributed by
North America, Latin America & Europe
Tuttle Publishing
364 Innovation Drive
North Clarendon, VT 05759-9436 U.S.A.
Tel: 1 (802) 773-8930; Fax: 1 (802) 773-6993
info@tuttlepublishing.com; www.tuttlepublishing.com

Japan
Tuttle Publishing
Yaekari Building 3rd Floor
5-4-12 Osaki Shinagawa-ku, Tokyo 141-0032
Tel: (81) 3 5437-0171; Fax: (81) 3 5437-0755
sales@tuttle.co.jp; www.tuttle.co.jp

Asia Pacific
Berkeley Books Pte. Ltd.
61 Tai Seng Avenue, #02-12, Singapore 534167
Tel: (65) 6280-1330; Fax: (65) 6280-6290
inquiries@periplus.com.sg; www.periplus.com

20 19 18 17   10 9 8 7 6 5 4 3 2 1
Printed in Hong Kong   1711EP

TUTTLE PUBLISHING® is a registered trademark of Tuttle Publishing,
a division of Periplus Editions (HK) Ltd.

AUTHOR'S NOTE
All Japanese names are given in the traditional order, with the family name first. As is customary, famous cultural figures are referred to by their given name, not their family name. Traditional Japanese architecture is subject to an ongoing process of addition and alteration, and it is often impossible to definitively state when a particular building was completed. Many dates (birth, deaths, constructions, demolitions, and so on) are still debated among historians. In each case, I have taken the most commonly accepted date, or that provided by the institution or family in question.